The Mobile

Marketing
Handbook

Advance Praise

"Savvy, down-to-earth and tremendously practical … if the price of this book were based on the value of the timeliness and thoroughness of the information it contains, it would sell for thousands of dollars."

—Ken McCarthy, CEO, The System Seminar

"*The Mobile Marketing Handbook* is a must have resource for marketing in the digital landscape. Kim Dushinski reveals exactly how to cash in on big brand mobile campaign results on any budget."

—Taylor Hunt, Head of Digital Promotion Development,
The Marketing Store, and Director of the 2008
McDonald's Monopoly Online/Mobile Game

"Building vs. buying? CPM vs CPC? Knowledge is vital for mobile advertising, and this book encapsulates not only what you need to know but how to capitalise as well."

—Bena Roberts, President, visibility mobile and GoMoNews.com

"Mobile marketing is not only the next frontier for the small business, it may become the only real way to get highly relevant messages in front of consumers. Kim Dushinski has tackled this subject as no one before her. You must understand this very practical topic to survive in business going forward."

—John Jantsch, author, *Duct Tape Marketing*

"Marketing professionals looking for a solid return on their investment using mobile marketing would be wise to follow the approach outlined by Kim Dushinski in *The Mobile Marketing Handbook*."

—Ajit Jaokar, futuretext

"You might be thinking, 'Why do I want to know about mobile marketing? I hate getting commercial messages on my cell!' But the kind of messaging that interrupts us, and ticks us off, is entirely old-school. So says author Kim Dushinski, in her excellent handbook. The new rules of mobile marketing are based less on interruption and more on offering people what they want, when they want it. Mobile isn't a technology, it's a way of life, and Dushinski helps marketers figure out how to use it well, and intelligently, to accomplish their business goals."

—Ann Handley, Chief Content Officer, MarketingProfs

"From legal issues to social media marketing, Kim Dushinski's *Mobile Marketing Handbook* covers the gamut of mobile marketing topics. If you read only one book on mobile marketing, this should be it."

—Janet Johnson, o'Johnson Partners

"Mobile marketing is the new Wild West. Very few people know what's going on out there, and most are shooting first and asking questions later. Kim Dushinski provides a terrific overview of the mobile web and specific ideas on mobile advertising, and she shows you where the gold mines are, as well as the snake oil salesmen. There's money to be made in mobile. Will your organization be a part of the new frontier?"

—David Meerman Scott, author, *The New Rules of Marketing & PR* and *Cashing in with Content*

"Dushinski has an incredible understanding of the mobile eco system. She takes a rather complex space and makes it easy enough for a novice to understand. *The Mobile Marketing Handbook* will help you craft many types of successful mobile marketing campaigns."

—Jared Reitzin, CEO, mobileStorm Inc.

"An excellent primer on mobile marketing. Whether you're new to the practice of mobile marketing, or you've been at it a while, you're sure to have a new and profound view regarding the power of the mobile channel and how it can be used for marketing after reading this book."

—Michael Becker, EVP Business Development, iLoop Mobile, Inc.

"In *The Mobile Marketing Handbook*, Kim Dushinski offers readers practical methods and tools to create compelling and engaging marketing campaigns for the remarkably challenging marketing environment that is now emerging on mobile phones. ... This book is desperately needed."

—Tomi T Ahonen, author, *Mobile as the 7th Mass Media Channel*

The Mobile Marketing Handbook

A Step-by-Step Guide to Creating DYNAMIC MOBILE MARKETING CAMPAIGNS

Kim Dushinski

Foreword by Laura Marriott

CyberAge Books

Information Today, Inc.
Medford, New Jersey

First printing, 2009

The Mobile Marketing Handbook: A Step-by-Step Guide to Creating Dynamic Mobile Marketing Campaigns

Copyright © 2009 by Kim Dushinski

A CIP catalog record for this book is available from the Library of Congress

Printed and bound in the United States of America

President and CEO: Thomas H. Hogan, Sr.
Editor-in-Chief and Publisher: John B. Bryans
Managing Editor: Amy M. Reeve
VP Graphics and Production: M. Heide Dengler
Project Editor: Barbara Brynko
Cover Design: Lisa Boccadutre
Book Design: Kara Mia Jalkowski
Proofreader: Bonnie Freeman
Indexer: Sharon Hughes

www.infotoday.com

What's with the Fish?

Almost everyone who saw the book cover in the design phase simultaneously loved it and then asked about the meaning of the fish jumping out of the phone. So here is what's with the fish:

- Marketers feel much the same as a fish out of water when trying to figure out mobile marketing. It is just too different from what they expect, and it keeps changing even when they think they have it figured out.

- To young people, having a mobile phone is part of life, and life is exciting. Mobile is always there for them and a part of being connected to the world. Why wouldn't a fish jump out of it?

- Mobile marketing brings phones to life in unexpected ways. Granted, no one would want a real fish to spring forth from his or her phone, but look at it as a metaphor for thinking outside the box about what you can do with your mobile device.

What do *you* think the fish means? Share your thoughts with me at kim@mobilemarketingprofits.com.

Contents

PART 1: MOBILE MARKETING STRATEGY AND IMPLEMENTATION

PART 2: MOBILE MARKETING TOOLBOX: TACTICS, CAMPAIGN IDEAS, AND RESOURCES

Acknowledgments

When I've read acknowledgments in other books, I thought the authors were exaggerating about how many people helped them. But that's not the case anymore. It is with complete gratitude and humbleness that I thank my family, friends, and colleagues who helped me with the book.

First, I would like to give John Bryans a momentous thank you for believing in me and saying "Yes" when I called him about writing a book. John, I especially appreciate your encouragement, constructive guidance, and sense of humor throughout the entire process. Thanks to Amy Reeve for helping me produce the best book possible. Amy, you are amazing. And thanks to Lisa Boccadutre for the awesome cover design, which I love so much. I am so grateful for your creativity. Rob Colding, it is great to work with you on the marketing. It's going to be a fun ride. And to Barbara Brynko, I am especially grateful that you accepted the call to be my Project Editor.

Peter Cranstone from 5o9 was the first to extend a hearty welcome to the mobile industry. Thanks for meeting me for tea so many times, for reading my first draft, and especially for encouraging me to take a giant leap and fill in the blanks later. And to Liz Coker, also from 5o9, for your early readings, help with some key concepts of mobile, and for coming to my first mobile marketing workshop. Through ForumOxford (an online community sponsored by the University of Oxford), I met many people, one of whom was Tomi Ahonen. Thank you so much, Tomi, for reading my rough draft (on a flight to China as I recall) and offering your unconditional support. I appreciate all the information you so graciously shared with me and thank you for giving me my first testimonial quote. To Victor Berggren, founder of MobileMarketing Watch, thanks for being my first mobile blogging friend and for giving me the opportunity to write on your blog.

There are so many other mobile industry folks I want to thank as well, but since I don't want to hear the equivalent of the Oscar music cutting off those long thank-you speeches, I will briefly thank the following people in no particular order (and please forgive me if I left anyone out): Chris Torbit, Blast Companies; Michael Becker, iLoopMobile; Faith McGary, InfoNXX, Inc.; Ajit Joakar, FutureText; William Volk, myNuMo; Greg Harris, Mobile Visions; Taylor Hunt, The Marketing Store; Cameron Doerty, Pocket Concierge; Adam Towvim, JumpTap; John Lauer, zipwhip; Doug Terfeher, Fleishman-Hillard International Communications; Gary Kibel, Davis & Gilbert LLP; Jared Reitzin, mobileStorm; Giff Gfroerer, i2SMS; Bena Roberts, GoMoNews; and Adam Boettiger, cmd. Talking with each of you helped me tremendously. I also want to thank Laura Marriott, of the Mobile Marketing Association, for her insights into mobile marketing.

A big thanks to Lauren Hasson, The Résumé Girl, for being my account-ability buddy, bounce-things-off-me person, and source of energy to keep me going. We're kindred spirits, for sure. To Kim Wolinski, thanks for read-ing chapters, encouraging me, and cheering me on. To my friend and long-time business partner, Tami DePalma, thanks for everything. Tami, your support as I ventured out on this journey without you has meant the world to me.

Thanks to both Ann Hession, my business coach, and Ponn Sabra, a blogging friend, for your empowering help.

I want to thank Ken McCarthy and his powerful System Seminar for teaching me about Internet marketing and for giving me the foundation of knowledge I needed to go into mobile marketing. Thanks for asking me to be a faculty member of The System; I am honored.

Thanks to Guaranty Bank in Golden, Colorado, for letting me have my first Mobile Marketing Workshop in the mountainview conference room and to everyone who attended and won a copy of this book by "texting to win."

Again to keep me from being too long winded, I'll thank my friends in groups: Book Club, Lucky Friends, MPHS friends, and the Gratitude Girls. My life and my book are better because of your friendship and support. Special thanks go to Vicki Espinoza for help with my math; it helps to know a "big gun" in accounting.

There are also online friends and colleagues who have helped me with this book. Thanks to everyone on ForumOxford, my Facebook friends, and the Twitterati. Special thanks to Peter Shankman for pushing me onto Facebook and to Zena Weist for pulling me into Twitter.

I want to thank all of my family for their support. Special thanks to my Uncle David for coming to my workshop even though you don't even own a cell phone, and to my brother-in-law Juan for flight privileges. To all my parents—Mom, Dad and Shirley, and Les and Myrna—thanks for being there when I needed you, for helping keep Anya entertained while I wrote, and for giving me an example of who I wanted to be when I grew up. To my sister, Julie, thanks for listening to me vent about how hard it is write a book and keep juggling everything else.

To my husband, Ken, thanks for your love and support all these years and the extra words of encouragement while I wrote the book. I'll never forget the licorice and the Subway lunch. Baby, you're the greatest. Anya, thank you for letting me rent your laptop, for being so patient while I was busy writing, and for cheering me on with my word count and color-coding. It means so much to know you believe in me.

Finally, thanks to our dogs, Luci and Dezi, who kept me company and my feet warm while I was writing.

Foreword

Anytime, anywhere, always on, always available ... mobile allows a brand to connect with the consumer like never before. A dialogue based on relevance, engagement, and consumer opt-in. For those who have participated in the Mobile Marketing Association or have heard me speak, this may sound like a broken record. I am one, in an industry of many passionate mobile advocates, hooked on mobile and the "power" of the mobile channel. Like many of my colleagues, I believe that mobile is positioned to emerge as the world's leading media and to become not the third screen, but the first screen for connecting the brand to the consumer.

With more than 3.3 billion handsets worldwide, compared to only 1 billion PCs, mobile is rapidly becoming the media of choice for consumers around the globe. Mobile provides access to the web when you're on the go, access to television or the Internet for populations where infrastructure is not yet deployed, and a means for a brand to create a relationship of affinity and interaction with its consumer. Mobile is a means to access the majority of the world's population in a highly contextual and relevant consumer driven interaction. How could we not be passionate about mobile?

I am often asked, "Is this is the year for mobile?" and, "If not, what is impeding the growth of broad scale mobile marketing adoption globally?"

Well, let's face it, mobile is here. We should stop trying to justify the answer to the question and, instead, start making it easier for those who want to engage and adopt to do just that. When I began leading the Mobile Marketing Association we focused heavily on the technology. A mobile campaign sale to a brand might first focus on conversations around cool technology—on "neat" demos, awesome platforms, and the "Wow" instead of the "How." We have now learned that the key to success is helping to define and achieve brand strategic objectives and leverage creativity and innovation, regardless of the technology we use, to achieve campaign success.

Impediments to growth have included perceptions that mobile marketing is intrusive for brands, agencies, and consumers alike. However, attitudes are beginning to shift globally, and brands increasingly understand what mobile can do to help extend their messages using a consumer opt-in driven model. There is also the perception that mobile is complicated. And, yes, while mobile may appear complex, the industry has come together to define terminology and create a streamlined means of market entry with simple, easy-to-follow guidelines and best practices that remove barriers and create a common platform on which to launch campaigns.

Just as marketers use traditional media to achieve varied marketing objectives, mobile must be considered a critical component within a larger cross media campaign. Integration of the mobile call to action into existing traditional and digital media spend is one of the critical lessons we have learned in deploying successful campaigns.

Richard Saggers, Head of Mobile Advertising for Vodafone Group Services, shares that for mobile marketing to be successful we must ensure cross media integration, relevance, perceived consumer benefit, engaging interaction, and—most importantly—that it is not intrusive. One of the obstacles to overcome is the perceived consumer belief that mobile marketing involves push-based initiatives (unsolicited communications) directed at this highly personal device on an ad-hoc basis. However, unlike email or the Internet, mobile marketing is permission-based and consumers are able to proactively select the initiatives they participate in.

Consumer acceptance will be paramount to growing mobile marketing spend. Today, the dollars for mobile marketing might be best characterized as "trial/test and learn" and, before allocating additional budget to mobile, brands require an understanding of the role mobile media plays in the overall mix, consumer acceptance of brand messaging, consistent guidelines and best practices, and evidence of effectiveness/value via consistent metrics, measurement, and reporting.

Thus, education is key to the growth of our industry—both on the agency and the client sides. The success of mobile marketing efforts will be maximized by educating consumers on the benefits they will realize from participation, and by educating brands on how to engage this channel in the right way.

A digital marketing agency told me, "Our biggest challenge right now is figuring out what mobile marketing offerings we're best positioned to assist our clients with. ... We need to assess where our value proposition will lie in mobile." Agencies are determining how they can expand their mobile offerings to help clients—and where and how they will find the expertise they need to succeed.

The Mobile Marketing Handbook: A Step-by-Step Guide to Creating Dynamic Mobile Marketing Campaigns provides this much-needed education. It is a must-read resource if you are contemplating launching a mobile initiative, or are simply looking to understand your options. The book helps readers grasp the challenges in defining objectives, choosing partners, and implementing tactics to achieve goals. And the information is delivered in an understandable and easy-to-use format.

The question of how to get started in mobile marketing is one I hear often, and this essential book is the kind of resource that will provide you with the insight you need to get involved—today. It will provide you with the basics and help you gain the knowledge to identify the important considerations for implementing your solution and achieving success.

A rising industry tide will float all ships, creating revenue for the brands and enhanced opportunities for the consumer. We will all win. Let's keep our campaigns simple and relevant, deliver on value to the consumer—and have fun! *The Mobile Marketing Handbook* is your start.

Laura Marriott
President
Mobile Marketing Association

About the Online Resource Guide
www.mobilemarketinghandbook.com

Mobile marketing is a new industry that changes quickly. In addition to the smart strategies and cutting-edge tools and techniques you'll find in this book, you can count on frequent updates, new vendors, and additional resources in the Online Resource Guide available at www.mobilemarketing handbook.com. Each chapter of the book has its own link, so you can go directly to updates, resources, and bonuses specifically associated with each chapter. For specifics, check out the Chapter Updates and Online Resource Guide and Resources sections at the end of each chapter.

Disclaimer

Neither the publisher nor the author makes any claim as to the results that may be obtained through the use of this website or of any of the Internet resources it references or links to. Neither publisher nor author will be held liable for any results, or lack thereof, obtained by the use of this page or any of its links; for any third-party charges; or for any hardware, software, or other problems that may occur as the result of using it. This website is subject to change or discontinuation without notice at the discretion of the publisher and author.

Introduction

If you are interested in mobile marketing, specifically in learning how to launch an effective mobile marketing campaign and get the best return on investment with it, you will find *The Mobile Marketing Handbook* useful. The step-by-step approach is specifically designed for marketing professionals and entrepreneurs who need practical advice on getting started with and/or improving mobile marketing campaigns. Within this book, you'll find everything from strategic decision making to tools and techniques like text messaging, mobile website creation, mobile promotion, and proximity marketing to use to market with mobile. Many of the companies used as examples and some of the vendors included as resources are North American, but it is important to note that the strategies and principles are applicable around the world.

My View of Mobile Marketing

Marketing has fascinated me ever since I worked part-time in marketing for a travel agency during college. At that time in the late 1980s, I wrote a small travel newsletter and typed it on a typewriter in columns. Then I would paste it up on blue line paper, cover the edges with Wite-Out so the lines didn't show, and drive the camera-ready copy to the printer. As part of my job as marketing director at the travel agency, I coordinated event nights, placed ads in the local paper, managed the database of client names, and worked to ensure the travel agents would track which one of my marketing efforts had brought in which client.

Even though I was planning to go to law school after graduation, I simply couldn't give up marketing when the time came. It was too much fun. Instead of applying to law school, I took out a small business loan to buy a computer, a laser printer, and WordPerfect software, and I launched a small business marketing/desktop publishing business. At that point, I had state-of-the-art equipment: My hard drive was the biggest available at 40 MB (now there are 32 GB USB flash drives), and my 300 dpi printer was the key to running my desktop publishing business. I remember getting a fax machine a few years later and feeling as though I had stepped into a new world. Suddenly, I could fax a draft to clients and not have to drive it across town myself or wait for their revisions in the mail.

Then along came email, which was a novelty at first. When I met someone at a networking event who had an email address listed on his or her business card, I was thrilled to find a kindred spirit who had also embraced this new technology. When I aligned with my business partner, Tami, and she moved into my one-room office, we shared an email address for a few years until we finally acquired our own domain name, a new office space, and our first employee in our book publicity firm.

One day when I was checking our email, I distinctly remember saying that "someday this is all going to be huge." I said that people would have their own email and that companies would be doing business online as a normal course of business. That was in 1995. And as it turns out, I was right.

I have the same sensation now about mobile marketing. It soon will be a normal course of business to have a mobile web presence and be in interactive touch with customers regularly via their mobile devices. It will be routine for people to use their mobiles for everything from jumping on the mobile web multiple times per day for a variety of reasons to getting downloaded content all the time wherever they are to purchasing physical goods to interacting with signs and other marketing all the time. Mobile is going to become more integrated into the lives of Americans and the marketing mix of businesses.

In the U.S., a few kindred spirits have jumped on board with the uses of their mobile devices beyond its phone capabilities, but most consumers and businesses are oblivious to what is coming. People say, "I don't even know how to send a text message" or "You can really go on the web on your phone?" or "I need to build a mobile website now, too?"

When Tami and I started creating and selling how-to-market-your-book information in addition to our book publicity services, we wrote a huge how-to-do book promotion notebook and bundled it with teleconferences to teach it. At the time (it was 1998), people didn't know what teleconferences were. People were puzzled: "You mean I will be on a call with other people at the same time? How does that work?" Now, teleconferencing is as normal as making a phone call, and webinars are a common way to have meetings with others in different offices, different cities, or even different countries.

Today, most companies haven't even started to consider a mobile web presence, they don't use text messaging as the powerful marketing tool it can be, and they don't run mobile publicity campaigns or sell physical goods via m-commerce. But companies need to consider a mobile web presence now. While there are many areas of disagreement within the mobile industry, everyone agrees on one thing: timing. It is time to jump on the mobile marketing bandwagon.

If you have any doubt about that, remember how fast we went from not even knowing what a website was to using the Internet in daily life? Remember when a business having a website was unique? Remember how the companies that jumped on board early with the Internet staked a claim and earned their fortunes? Remember how quickly new technology such as the fax machine, email, and teleconferences became integrated into daily business life?

Mobile is the next new technology, and it is coming quickly. Around the world, Japan, Korea, and Spain are several years ahead of us in adopting and using mobile devices in daily life. A fascinating book about this is *Digital Korea* by Tomi T Ahonen and Jim O'Reilly (futuretext, 2007). Businesses in Asia and Europe are already moving forward in the new marketing era. While the development and use of mobile technology is still in its formative stages here in North America, there is still time to be one of the first businesses to take advantage of this new technology. But there is no time to wait if you want to take advantage of using this powerful new marketing tool.

That is exactly why I moved into mobile marketing. When it became apparent that I needed a change from book promotion, I decided to find a place in marketing that was new and exciting with an open place to help businesses. Mobile fit the bill. It is the newest marketing tool, and each day brings something exciting in mobile. Since everything is changing, there is ample opportunity for me to help people get moving with mobile. I love it.

The basic components of marketing haven't changed much since my early days at the travel agency. Events are still coordinated, databases are still gathered, news is still distributed to customers, and staff members with direct customer contact still have to help with tracking. But the marketing tools certainly have changed. We've gone from typewriters to text messages in 20 years. The next round of changes will go much faster. While it took 10 years for the Internet to become a mainstay of daily life, it will probably take only three to four years for mobile marketing to be so commonplace that we as businesses and consumers will have a tough time remembering what life was like without it, much the same as TV, email, and the Internet are now.

Who Will Benefit from This Book and How

The strategies and techniques in this book will help anyone who is doing mobile marketing learn how to strategize a campaign and launch it. It is designed for practical use by marketers using mobile as a marketing tool. While many statistics, examples, and vendors in the book are North American, the principles of mobile marketing and the step-by-step tactics are globally applicable.

Marketing Professionals

Whether you work at an agency or in-house at a company, you already know about marketing strategies but just need to know how to fit mobile into the marketing mix. This book will show you all the details of mobile and how to integrate mobile into your current marketing, a process that will make your current marketing all that more effective. Dive in; you're going to love mobile marketing.

Why Is Mobile Marketing Different from Other Marketing?

Since you are already a marketing expert, you will be tempted to assume that mobile is the same as all your other marketing. While many of the strategic concepts are the same, mobile as a marketing tool is unique. Specifically, it requires providing value to your target market for it to work to its true potential as a marketing tool. It is also not the same as TV or the Internet but only smaller. You must consider other factors such as how personal the device is to the person to whom you are marketing. No other media is physically located so continuously close to each individual user—most people have their cell phones with them all the time. How your audience interacts with your marketing is also completely different because they have to decide to participate in your campaign; it doesn't just come to them. Where your audience is when you are marketing to them is a critical component of your campaign. Make no mistake about it, mobile is different. This book will show you how it is different and how to use it as an effective marketing tool.

Businesses with a Business-to-Consumer Focus

Mobile marketing is certainly a great tool for big businesses, but it is not just for Fortune 500 companies and household brand names. In fact, small and medium-sized businesses are an ideal match for mobile marketing, especially with local marketing. As you will see, location-specific information is the No. 1 search that people seek on their mobile devices. Local businesses can use mobile as a powerful marketing tool. Fortunately, just as tools and vendors are matched for the needs of Corporate America, there are also resources that work for small and medium-sized businesses. This book will offer ways to choose which marketing tool is the best to integrate first, based on your customers and your needs. It will also show you step-by-step how to launch your mobile marketing strategy. Almost any business that markets to consumers can find a way to market with mobile.

Businesses with a Business-to-Business Focus

In most situations, using mobile effectively in a business-to-business (B2B) environment will be more difficult than business-to-consumer (B2C). However, mobile will work well for certain B2B marketing. Any event setting, such as a trade show or conference, is likely to be a good opportunity to work with mobile to reach your audience, especially if your mobile campaigns are specifically tied to events and not used otherwise. It is also possible that launching a mobile marketing campaign at these events will let you proceed with mobile other times as well.

Will Mobile Work for Your Target Market or Your Business?

I am frequently asked whether mobile marketing will work for a particular business. And my answer is that it all depends upon two factors: whether you can find something of value to provide to your customers via mobile, and whether your customers are generally mobile-savvy. In later chapters, we'll take a look at ways to provide value for your customers in great detail, but for now, just fill out the "Mobile-Savvy Worksheet" in Chapter 1, which will give you a good indication of how likely it is that mobile marketing will work for you.

Entrepreneurs

If you are thinking about starting a mobile-based business, this book can show you how. It is not written with that exact premise in mind, but if you read it with that mind-set, you will see what to do. This will be especially true if you are already an Internet marketer. Many of the concepts will already be familiar, and this book will give you the specifics that are unique to mobile. Be aware that technologies and abilities to "build your own solution" will likely not work as expected on the Internet. For example, you cannot simply create and launch a text message service on your own. You will need to deal with carriers, aggregators, and other companies as you proceed. This may be a bit of shock to you since you can probably do anything you like on the Internet. One bit of advice though: If you want to take the lead ahead of the pack in mobile, don't wait. Take action now. This is much the same as having knowledge of Internet marketing in 1995 when no one else did. Stake your claim quickly so you don't miss the opportunity.

How This Book Is Organized

Smart marketing always starts with strategy and then moves into tactics and tools. This book is designed to lead you through the steps for developing a sound mobile marketing strategy first, and then it will discuss the tools to implement your strategy. Part 1, Mobile Marketing Strategy and Implementation, is a solid introduction to mobile marketing: what it is and whether it will work for your business. This section will guide you in orchestrating a smart strategy for your mobile campaign. It includes the Smart Mobile Marketing Matrix, which is an essential tool for planning your mobile campaign. With this matrix, you can create a mobile campaign that works for your business and your customers. Part 1 also covers implementation: what you need to know to start and who to contact for what you'll need. Part 2, Mobile Marketing Toolbox: Tactics, Campaign Ideas, and Resources, discusses the tactics and tools available via mobile. You'll learn which tools to use now while everything mobile is new for consumers and what you can put in the plan to implement later when mobile marketing is more common. Each chapter will cover what the marketing tool is and when and how to use it and will give you resources and some working examples.

Since mobile marketing can be used by anyone or anything that uses marketing, this book is written for all types and sizes of businesses, companies, nonprofits, groups, and entrepreneurs. I use the words *business* and *company* interchangeably to mean any type of entity. I often use the word *you* when I am speaking about the business involved in mobile marketing, which comes from my entrepreneurial roots where the line between business and owner is blurred. Similarly, I will talk about *customers*, *clients*, and *target markets* to mean the end user with whom your business wishes to conduct business. Likewise, instead of using mobile phone, I will use often use *mobile device*, which includes all types of cell phones, from basic phones to smartphones and gaming devices. There are certain instances where I use the term *cell phone*. When I do, that means I am speaking specifically about cell phones and no other type of mobile device. As mobile technology forges ahead, the fact that it is a phone will be increasingly less important than that it is mobile. Throughout the book, I use 12345 as an example of short code (the number used in text messaging). This is the equivalent of using a 555 phone number, since 12345 is not a valid short code. Lastly, you will find that my writing style is more casual in tone than most business books. I'm not likely to use corporate-ese when plain English works just fine. This will be helpful since the other information in the mobile industry is highly technical.

Since mobile is new and unfamiliar to many people, I have included a Glossary, which may come in handy if there are terms with which you aren't familiar. Additionally, there is a Resource section at the end of each chapter that includes other books to read, vendors to use to implement your campaign, and various other items that will help you as you launch your campaigns. There is also an Online Resource Guide (www.mobilemarketinghandbook.com), which, includes chapter updates and useful tools.

Throughout the book, I have showcased companies that are doing mobile marketing campaigns. I certainly appreciate these mobile marketing pioneers forging the path for us to follow. You will find that you'll learn from their stories (successes and failures) as you do from my how-to advice. But you'll find that you learn the most from diving in with your own campaigns after you finish the book. So, I suggest that you get to work creating your own example.

Mobile Marketing Strategy and Implementation

Often when mobile marketing is discussed, the focus is about its technology: what a certain handset can do, how cell phone carriers are implementing a service, the specific behind-the-scenes details of mobile web design, what mobile operating system can accomplish a certain task, or even how the technology of certain mobile tools works. Of course, all of these are important foundations of mobile, but the truth is that technology doesn't matter to the mobile marketer when it comes time to develop a meaningful campaign. What matters most is developing a strategy that will use a technology to accomplish a specific end result. The chapters in Part 1 focus on the strategic development and implementation of mobile marketing campaigns.

From the material in the first two chapters, "The Basics and the Big Picture" and "Five Steps to Creating a Dynamic Mobile Marketing Campaign," you will find out how to create a solid foundation for your campaigns. You'll see clearly how and why you need to integrate mobile into your other marketing methods to create the most successful campaigns. In

Chapter 3, information about legal issues and implications will help you get your mobile campaign smoothly through your legal department. Then, Chapters 4, 5, and 6 cover the meat and potatoes of launching, marketing, and tracking your campaign.

As tempting as it may be to skip this part and jump right to the fun and exciting tools found in the Mobile Marketing Toolbox in Part 2, resist the urge. Without the smart marketing strategies found in Part 1, you run the risk of launching a less-than-perfect mobile marketing campaign, alienating your customers, not knowing what is working with your campaign, and ultimately wasting money, or perhaps even getting in trouble with the law. So it's well worth learning all about the basics first.

The Basics and the Big Picture

No matter how mobile advertising messages are delivered, our research shows that consumers demand that if a company is going to invade their personal space with advertising, it better be for something of interest to them. Personalization is hyper-critical.

—Judith Ricker, division president, Harris Interactive

What Is Mobile Marketing Anyway?

Businesses and their brands can reap big rewards from mobile marketing if it's done right. When mobile marketing is done right, you can reach your customers via mobile with a message they actually want from you. You can deliver a message to your customers that they are actually waiting for but might not know it yet. And the real kicker is that your customers will reach out and even ask you for a message.

But maybe I'm getting ahead of myself. Perhaps I should explain what mobile marketing is *not*. Contrary to what many consumers worry about (and what shady opportunists fantasize about), mobile marketing is not a barrage of unwanted text messages sent to the cell phone of someone who may not want, need, or have any connection with the business sending the messages. That's just spam.

The Mobile Marketing Association (MMA) defines mobile marketing as: "The use of wireless media (primarily cellular phones and PDAs) as an integrated content delivery and direct response vehicle within a crossmedia marketing program."

My definition of mobile marketing is a bit different: *Mobile marketing connects businesses and each of their customers (through their mobile devices) at the right time and at the right place with the right message and requires the customer's explicit permission and/or active interaction.* Based on this definition, marketing to groups who may or may not be interested in receiving your message is not smart mobile marketing. Instead, smart mobile marketing is all about reaching your customers or potential customers one at a time in a way that adds value to their day. You've undoubtedly noticed that the basic foundation of my definition is permission. Mobile marketing will never work as an invasive marketing method and should not be undertaken in that way under any circumstances. It's likely to backfire every time. When mobile is used as a marketing tool, it must be done with explicit permission by the end user or it will fail. Any mobile outreach that is done without permission not only impacts the business doing it, but it also casts a negative light on the entire industry. (Clearly, this does not eliminate mobile web advertising because anyone who goes online, even with a mobile device, naturally assumes that advertising will be interwoven with content somewhere.)

Mobile Devices Defined

Mobile devices can be any type of cell phone from basic flip phones to more elaborate smartphones to iPhones. They can also be PDAs (personal digital assistants) or Tablet PCs (portable computers that are smaller than laptops). Even gaming units such as Sony's hand-held game device PSPs (PlayStation Portables) are considered mobile devices because they can access the Internet through Wi-Fi and are often used away from home. For the most part in this book, we will be discussing marketing to consumers through their cell phones, but remember there are many ways to market to consumers via mobile. For your reference, when the phrase "cell phone" is used, I am referring specifically to cell phones and not mobile devices universally. When I use the term "mobile devices," I'm including cell phones and other types of devices as well.

With mobile, a business has the chance of interacting with customers at any time but only if customers agree. Customers can pick up their cell phones to request a text message when they're out or even at home watching TV or reading a magazine. Customers can search on their mobile devices to find your mobile website. They can also call your business spontaneously wherever they are. Soon your customers will be able to use their phones to track where they are. Then you can combine that information with any preferences they have already indicated and offer the right marketing based on where they are and what they are interested in receiving. If done correctly, mobile marketing will soon be so deeply interwoven in people's daily lives that they really won't be able to imagine life without it.

While consumers have always been able to respond directly to advertising, it has never been so fluid and so immediate. The majority of those who use mobile devices have them at all times, even while they're driving, walking down the street, shopping, or even sleeping. Most will go back for the device if they leave it at home. While we all know someone who only has a mobile device "for emergencies" or those who claim "I never turn mine on," most people have their phones with them and turned on at all times. Because of mobile use, your customers can and will choose to interact with you at any given moment. The key to a successful mobile marketing campaign is to make your customers want to interact with you. That's what this book is all about. If you can create a mobile marketing campaign that makes people want to interact with your business, then you will be well on the road to success.

Many marketers mistakenly regard the mobile marketing environment as a smaller version of the Internet or similar to TV but simply consumed in smaller doses by viewers. That isn't the case. Mobile is more than its own unique marketing channel; it is a unique mass media. As print, recording, radio, cinema, TV, and the Internet that came before it, mobile has its own characteristics that make it a mass media. Even as the newest mass media, it is the most widespread media worldwide, it is the most personal (giving it the ability to closely target individuals and not general demographics), and it is always on and has a built-in payment mechanism. (See a more detailed examination of this topic in the Appendix at the end of the book.)

But mobile is unlike television because its content (and your marketing) is consumed by one individual at a time. It is unlike the Internet because people interact with the mobile web differently, using a much smaller interface than on a full-size computer. They find; they don't browse. And the big difference is that people are usually on the go when they are using mobile. Marketers must keep their customers' location in mind when creating campaigns. The better aligned your campaign is with what your customers want and where they are, the more successful you'll be.

Marketers also often underutilize mobile. You can make your complete, full-size website render reasonably well on most mobile devices by miniaturizing it, but is that really what your customers want? Some see mobile as the ultimate brand-awareness tool. And while you can use mobile marketing for branding, it is not the most comprehensive use. That's much the same as buying a Ferrari and only driving it 20 mph to church once a week. It is a waste of potential. This book can help you tap into the full potential of mobile as a marketing tool.

Opportunities in Mobile Marketing

If you don't use your mobile device all the time and can't see how businesses can easily engage you via mobile, you may be wondering if this is a viable marketing strategy. Maybe you have been charged with launching a mobile campaign and justifying the return on investment (ROI) for the marketing budget allocated toward mobile. Either way, you should know that the mobile marketplace is big and getting bigger. More than 3 billion people now have mobile phones worldwide. That translates to almost half the world's population. When you consider this mobile adoption figure rate includes the young and the elderly who are not typical cell phone users, this statistic is truly amazing. Even more astonishing is that hubs around the world, including Hong Kong, Taiwan, Singapore, Italy, and Israel, have a cell phone usage rate of more than 100 percent since many residents have more than one phone.

Since this book is primarily aimed at the North American market, it is helpful to know that usage in the U.S. has just crossed the 80 percent mark. In early 2008, more than 250 million of the 303 million residents in the U.S. have a cell phone. At the end of 2007, there were almost 20 million cell phone subscribers in Canada, which represents a 60 percent penetration rate.

This statistic reflects two factors. First, North America is still lagging behind many parts of Asia and Europe in adopting mobile. This is useful because we can look at these mobile leaders for trends in the mobile space. Interestingly, the exact opposite happened with the Internet, as the U.S. was ahead of the curve in adopting that technology. Second, even if we are lagging behind in adopting mobile technology compared to our neighbors around the world, mobile users still represent a huge market. The next time you are in a public place, look around and see how many people have a cell phone or other mobile device. Many people around you will be actively using their mobile devices making calls, looking online, sending a text message, checking email, adjusting their calendars, taking pictures, or even listening to music. If the people in your line of sight are not actively using a phone, they probably have one strapped on their belt, tucked into their purse, or are holding one in their hand. Compare this to how many of the same people are reading or carrying a newspaper, magazine, radio, or television. Mobile is the only media that offers this level of continuous inter-connectivity to individuals in their daily lives.

But there's one word of caution. Even if people use their mobile devices this much, it does not mean that they are waiting for marketing campaigns to be delivered to them on this highly personal device. It simply means there is an opportunity for you to reach your customers more easily and more personally than ever before, and likewise, it means your customers have a way to reach you more easily than ever before. They have a way of connecting to your business and each other directly or indirectly at all times. You just need to give them the opportunity to engage with your business via mobile. It may be easier than you think.

When other advertising/marketing mediums first started, there was a similar high-response rate that is partially due to the novelty of the method. Arguably, TV ads in the 1950s worked well because they were new, and consumers were not inundated with ads that were considered to be part of the new TV experience. Mobile is that way now. It is a novelty to vote someone off a TV show, request a text message for more information or a discount, or watch a video on the mobile web. While it is difficult to document how many text messages users actually read, the numbers are high because people typically do not skip messages. Text messages have been documented as getting a buying response rate of 13 percent. Click-through rates (CTRs) for mobile web advertising are now 3 percent to 6 percent, but they have been known to reach as high as 19 percent. In contrast, Internet banner ad CTRs can often be less than 1 percent. As mobile marketing becomes more relevant to the consumer, mobile ad CTRs are likely to climb even higher.

But what do I mean by mobile marketing becoming more relevant? Imagine a consumer pulling into the parking lot of her favorite shopping center and automatically getting a text message with a link to the shopping center's mobile website. Of course, she would have previously requested the information. The link wouldn't just connect to the shopping center's generic mobile website; rather, she would receive a customized page that features timely information about what is going on in the mall. When she originally signed up for this mobile campaign, she specified the stores she shops at the most at this mall. Naturally, her favorites appear first on her customized mobile page with special coupons, offers, loyalty programs, and events that day. Before she sets foot in the mall, she has opened a text message she requested, went to a mobile site, and mapped her shopping trip at her favorite stores. Quite possibly, she will be drawn into one of her favorite stores that she might have walked by that day because she found out about a special offer or an event. Maybe the offer was double loyalty points valid that day only in a particular store that she just couldn't pass up. The mall can also tempt her to visit other stores based on the online principle of "If you like this store, you'll probably also like this one." In this example, the entire experience is relevant to her, and the response rate for the participating stores will reflect the usefulness to the customer. This scenario is similar to receiving one of those value coupon packages in the mail, but this time, the coupons are only for the stores she wants and are hand delivered when she stopped near the stores. Do you see the difference in the relevance to the consumer? The response rate from the customer increases as the offer becomes more beneficial to the consumers when they need it.

In theory, the first mall that creates this kind of mobile ad campaign in its market area can revolutionize the shopping experience. Customers are likely to take advantage of this unique marketing because it is new and exciting. As more malls begin to employ this tactic, it can become a customary way of doing business; it will more likely become so ingrained in how people shop that they can't imagine heading off to the mall without it.

Businesses that jump into the mobile marketing arena now have the advantage of being new and exciting. This advantage is a once-in-a-lifetime opportunity. But once people are used to mobile marketing, they will become more discerning about what mobile campaigns they will use. Think of your own online habits when you subscribe to email newsletters. When offers for email newsletters first started popping up, you probably subscribed to any one you found. Now, you probably think carefully before you subscribe to another. So you certainly want to be involved when the customers are beginning to participate in mobile campaigns. Mobile will eventually become so integrated into daily life that you'll want your business to be part of it. By being one of the frontrunners in the arena, you can grab people's interest early and become an essential part of their mobile online experience.

How Big Is the Mobile Market?

Ironically, mobile is the most global marketing tool and the most local at the same time. While more than 3 billion people worldwide have mobile access, many of these people with cell phones still don't have desktop Internet access, TV, or even newspapers. Yet, these people in far away lands may not be your customers. A local business may only want to reach people within a 25-mile radius. Still, that local audience may be accessible through mobile in a way they are not in any other medium.

For example, the Denver metro area has a population of 2.7 million people; 80 percent of the population (2.16 million residents) are cell phone subscribers who likely have their phones on and with them all the time every day. The Denver Newspaper Agency's advertising material states that an ad in its Sunday paper reaches 1.4 million readers on its highest circulation day. Furthermore, only 7 out of 10 adults read at least one newspaper once a week, according to the agency. Even though TV use in households is practically universal, TV advertising usually isn't viable for a specific local campaign. With radio, reaching a wide range of your customer base means that you need to advertise on a large number of stations to reach your audience. Within any 25-mile radius, there may simply be no better way to reach as many people in your target market than mobile. Granted, you have to work to get the people in your market area to interact with your mobile platform, but once you do, you have established a relationship with your customer on mobile that is unique compared to any other advertising or marketing you can undertake.

In addition to the sheer number of consumers who have mobile access, there is the growing investment in mobile marketing by advertisers. A white paper by Juniper Research titled *Mobile Advertising—Because I'm Worth It* estimates that "total annual adspend on mobile services will exceed $1 billion for the first time during 2008, and that over the course of the year it will reach $1.3 billion, rising to nearly $7.6 billion by 2013. This represents an average annual growth rate of 42%."

Why You Need to Take Action Now, Even If You're Not Ready

Mobile marketing is growing quickly. Being one of the first in your industry or your neighborhood to create a mobile marketing campaign will give you the advantage. You will be able to grab a good share of the audience because you'll be one of the first to break ground on the process.

See the Mobile Web in Action

If you want to see visual proof that people around the world are consuming the mobile web and all it has to offer, check out Bango Analytics Live (www.bango.com/live). You can watch the mobile web in action. This site shows a live sample of people worldwide using their mobile phones to browse websites, interact with ads or marketing campaigns, and even buy downloadable content. You may have to scroll down to see it, but check the continually updated list of handsets and what they are doing. Seeing this continuous scrolling screen of mobile buyers in action gives you a sense of the scope of reach with mobile and the level of actual buying activity.

For example, let's say you own a restaurant in a neighborhood, and you start a text message campaign to alert people about Two-for-One nights (those slower nights when you could use more people coming in the door). On slow nights, you will have a tool to get more customers, and your competitors won't. The same thing holds true with the mobile web. If you have a mobile website and your competitors don't, you are ahead of the game. The best way to do that is to get going now.

As with any new technology, there will be kinks to work out as you undertake mobile marketing. If you get your game plan established now, you will be ready to help your customers with a mobile website as the market continues to grow. Your competition may still be trying to figure it out. So take steps into the mobile marketing world as quickly as possible.

Why Mobile Now Is Like the Internet Was in 1997 (and Why It's Not)

The emergence of mobile as a highly integrated consumer device is now similar to what the Internet was in 1997, especially in North America. Early adopters who use mobile and those who use it as a marketing tool are similar to those who jumped on the Internet when it first appeared. However, many people may think the process of going online using their phone is a completely foreign concept. "You can go online on your phone?" Millions of consumers still think of text messaging as something that only young people do and have no intention of doing it themselves. Don't worry, there were also many people who thought the Internet was a fad and that it wouldn't last.

However, the emergence of mobile marketing is different in that the adoption cycle is faster. In fact, more people worldwide were said to have accessed Internet content on phones than from desktop computers in 2007. As author Tomi T Ahonen states in *Thought Piece: Understanding the 7th Mass Media*, "This is no mere sci-fi fantasy of technology buffs; it has already happened in Japan, South Korea and China by 2006." Mobile use by consumers is growing fast worldwide; according to Ahonen, users sent 2.8 trillion text messages in 2007, and the short message service (SMS) industry generates $100 billion a year.

Marketing with mobile now is also different from marketing with the Internet in 1997 because marketers already have a working knowledgebase. Businesses took years to figure out that the Internet was more like direct mail than TV. We can use that knowledgebase to figure out how to market with mobile effectively more quickly than we did with the Internet. In fact, many of the technologies, including mobile search and mobile advertising, are similar to their Internet counterparts. Yet, they are distinct services and technologies with an uncluttered landscape.

Mobile as a medium is not like the Internet in other ways. Consumer use of mobile is already inundated. People use mobile already; they just need to begin to interact with businesses via mobile. With the Internet's emergence, people had to learn about the Internet and the World Wide Web to begin using it. Remember when people used to say, "Go to H-T-T-P colon back slash back slash w-w-w dot" and then list the website name? There was a big learning curve for consumers who had to be convinced to use the Internet at all. Now, people already know how to use their cell phones, and they have already been through the Internet learning curve. Plus, there is an entire generation of consumers who have grown up with mobile as an integrated part of their lives and don't need any lessons at all; they just need to be presented with the right offer at the right time. Mobile marketing is weaving its way into society more quickly than the Internet did.

How Mobile-Savvy Is Your Audience?

Clearly, knowing that your customer base can be reached via a mobile platform is the key to being able to proceed with mobile marketing. You can figure this out in several different ways. First, assume that your customers are mobile-savvy if you sell to one of the early adopter markets in mobile, such as people under 30 and/or corporate data plan users (corporate employees with company-paid cell phones that typically have the most comprehensive packages for cell phone use). To figure out if you have customers who use mobile extensively, you can use an informal survey to find out in a couple of ways: First, observe your customers to see who uses cell phones or other mobile devices in and around your place of business or send a survey in your newsletter or via email asking your customers if they use mobile, and if so for what. You can also ask customers, as they are paying for their goods or services or handling some other routine interaction, if they use mobile phones for anything other than phone calls.

Try answering the questions in Figure 1.1 to help you figure out if you have a mobile-savvy audience ready for a mobile marketing campaign. If you answer "Yes" to question No. 1 in the worksheet, your market is most assuredly mobile-savvy. Using this book as your guide, you can proceed with any and all mobile marketing techniques included here that fit into your marketing mix and your particular target market. You'll be able to work with some of the more advanced tools such as proximity marketing or social networking, both of which will be explained in depth in later chapters, if you so choose. Don't feel like you have to use these techniques, though; the

Mobile-Savvy Worksheet

❶ Is your target market primarily under age 30?

YES   NO

❷ Is your target market likely to have a company-paid-for cell phone with a data plan? (*This would be salespeople, upper-level management, people who work for a major corporation, etc.*)

YES   NO

❸ Can you find at least 5 mobile websites that would be of interest to your target market? (*Do a few searches on mobile search engines. Search on the mobile web if you can.*)

YES   NO

❹ If you survey 100 customers and ask if they use their mobile phone for *anything else besides making phone call*, do at least 50 to 60 of them say yes?

YES   NO

❺ Is a big percentage of your market non-recently immigrated Hispanics?

YES   NO

❻ Is you target market an easily definable niche–are there trade shows, magazines, and blogs targeted specifically toward your audience?

YES   NO

Figure 1.1   Answering the questions on this worksheet can help you figure out if you have a mobile-savvy audience ready for a mobile marketing campaign.

tried-and-true options such as text messaging will still work well with your mobile-savvy market.

If you answer "No" to question No. 1 but answer "Yes" to at least three of the remaining questions, you can proceed with mobile marketing under one condition: Stick to the strategies that are easier to implement and the more widely accepted mobile uses such as text messaging and a basic mobile website for now.

If you answer "No" to question No. 1 and can't answer "Yes" to at least two of the remaining questions, your target market is probably not ready for mobile marketing yet. However, you can always try a simple text message campaign to verify this, or you can start to educate your customers about mobile to get them ready. It may not take your customers long to become mobile-savvy, so revisit your assessment of your target market frequently.

Remember, this worksheet only covers whether your target market is ready for mobile. The next hurdle is whether you have the right reason for them to want to interact with you via mobile. We'll go over this concept in detail in Chapter 2, when we discuss what value you can provide to your customers via mobile.

Who Is Using Mobile Now—The Savvy Markets

Consider some of the savvy groups of mobile consumers. Obviously, first and foremost is the younger crowd who have grown up with a cell phone (94 percent of the under-30 crowd have a cell phone) and can't imagine life without it. The 76 million Gen Y/Millennials (the under-30 crowd) are the prime market for mobile marketing. But this is also the same generation that is wary of advertising, marketing, and anything commercial. You will need to provide solid value to this market to get them engaged and to over-come their natural skepticism toward marketing. You will find that reaching them via mobile will be more about fun, entertainment, and connection than efficiency or making life easier. This group will be the easiest to get involved in the technology of your campaign because they already know how to use it. But they may be the least responsive if your marketing starts to feel like old-school advertising in any way.

Another engaged group of consumers is the business data plan users. These are executives and business people who have a smartphone and data plan provided by their companies so they can stay connected with work at all times. These men and women, made up of Gen Xers (in their 30s) and Baby Boomers, travel frequently or have high-tech needs that their mobile devices provide. They are a good market because they have the best devices and the best data plans. They have the smartphone to use and the data plan to make it affordable. However, they probably see their phones as business tools and may not want to be interactive when they don't have to be. By the time the workday is over, the last thing they may want to do is spend more time on their mobile devices. That said, there are plenty of ways to provide value to the market, especially as it helps them get through the workday as quickly and efficiently as possible. You may have to provide some education about how and why to engage with mobile to get them involved.

The third active group in mobile is Latinos. This is one of the most active cell phone user groups, according to a December 2007 study by Pew Internet & American Life Project that found that 84 percent of English-speaking Hispanics have cell phones. The study also reported that 56 percent of this population did some activity daily on their cell phones that involved sending or receiving data (text messaging, taking a picture, playing a game or music, and so on). Younger and more acculturated Hispanics use the Internet and wireless phones more frequently than Spanish-dominant and older adults. According to the study, Latinos are more likely to have only a cell phone (and no landline) and use plenty of cell phone minutes, and are less likely to have computer-based Internet access. Whatever the age ranges, Latinos are a prime market to consider in mobile marketing. Remember they are generally family oriented and love to connect and socialize. Consider too that not all Hispanics are from Mexico and that people who were born here or whose families have been here for multiple generations are quite different from recent immigrants. The level of acculturation makes a huge difference in market strategies for this demographic. For example, coupon use designed to increase product trials increases dramatically within the acculturated Hispanic population, with 62.5 percent of this group more likely to try a new product when a coupon is offered. But the coupon swayed only 41.4 percent of unacculturated Hispanics. The point here is to realize that while the Latino market is large, many segmented markets are included within this group. Be sure to pay attention to this fact when you build your campaigns.

Who Will Be Using Mobile Soon—The Upcoming Markets

Busy women will undoubtedly be the next big market opening up to mobile marketing. Many of them are already part of the under-30 crowd and/or the corporate data plan market, but the use of mobile to keep components (business, family, personal, and kids) in their busy lives organized will quickly drive this market to the forefront. Who needs the convenience of mobile more than a busy woman wearing many hats during the day? One thing that keeps them from being a more active market is the shortage of mobile websites and other mobile services dedicated to their needs. If you can be among the first to help this market with mobile, you can reap great rewards. Don't forget that women are the primary buying force in America and reaching this powerful group via mobile could certainly prove worthwhile. Don't expect this market to stay underserved for long. Major brands, such as Suave, are reaching out to this market with its collection of haircare products using a video series called "In the Motherhood" (www.inthemother hood.com), which can be seen online and on SprintTV. Likewise, Hearst Media Corporation is putting several of its magazines (*Redbook, House Beautiful,* and *Good Housekeeping*) on the mobile web.

Small-business owners are also likely to become good targets for mobile marketing campaigns. Business owners with busy lives will soon have the opportunity to make life easier via mobile. One example of mobile reaching this group is Wells Fargo Bank, which actively markets its mobile banking platform to small businesses: "Wells Fargo has announced the latest addition to its mobile banking services, Wells Fargo Mobile for small businesses, a browser-based solution that gives small business owners nationwide access to their business and personal financial information at anytime, from anywhere." Media outlets picked up this press announcement when Wells Fargo launched its mobile banking platform.

Niche markets, or those that align themselves by interest, are another prime target for mobile marketing initiatives. A niche market can include people who belong to a particular association, subscribe to a certain magazine, or work in a specific industry. Because there is a built-in way to reach this group, it is a good match for mobile marketing if you can provide a significant value to them via mobile. For example, mobile marketing can be used as a direct response tool at an industry trade show where everyone is gathered and interested in the same things. The results could be the same as shooting fish in a barrel for the right campaign.

The Big Picture

There is a legend about an artist who was asked whether it was easier to draw a dog or a demon. He said that it is easier to draw a demon because everyone knows what a dog is supposed to look like, so any errors in the drawing are obvious to everyone concerned. However, as a mythological creature, a demon could look like anything. So an artist can draw it however he likes, and no one can really find any fault. When I heard this story as part of an introduction by Justin Oberman of mopocket.com before a Mobile Web Americas conference, I was immediately struck by how true it is for mobile marketing. We have tools for both dogs and demons; it is up to clever marketers to figure out which one is best to create for any given campaign.

Creating a mobile marketing campaign is much like drawing a mythological creature. While it is easy to create a fun, elaborate, and highly technical campaign on paper, it may not be as easy to implement it in real life. While technology is just starting to come up to speed, some ideas are cost prohibitive to implement. Or perhaps providing the necessary education to get consumers to participate may curtail some of the potential return on investment of the campaign. It is still important to dream big and draw the demon, because even if technology is not ready for your idea yet, it soon will be. And you may just be surprised to find out that what you want to do is already possible with existing technology. The marketers who take risks to create campaigns that are new and bold are likely to reap the biggest rewards.

On the other hand, marketers who don't want to create something new or tremendously bold can stick to drawing dogs. There are plenty of mobile marketing artists who have gone before you, so you can model your campaign after a known entity. There is still ample room to launch solid campaigns that bring a nice return without using completely new and untried ideas.

For your benefit, I have organized Part 2 of this book so the easiest technologies to implement (the dogs) are explored first. Later in the book, I have included tools that are more futuristic (the demons), even if that future is coming quickly. This way, you know which artist's shoes you are stepping into so you can plan your strategies accordingly.

So what is the big picture for you? Mobile marketing can take a one-dimensional, deadbeat ad and turn it into a hyper-responsive marketing tool. Almost any business can jump into the mobile world and make a difference in its bottom line with an effective mobile marketing campaign. All it takes is creativity and a campaign that is designed around your customers' wants and needs. Mobile campaigns work quickly, and the response can be phenomenal if you stay focused on the customers' needs. This book can guide you through all the steps, generate ideas, and put the tools into your hands to build truly dynamic mobile marketing campaigns.

Chapter Updates and Online Resource Guide

Updates to this chapter and its related Online Resource Guide are available at www.mobilemarketinghandbook.com/Updates/BigPicture.

The Online Resource Guide for Chapter 1 includes links for all sites listed in this chapter.

Resources

The following resources are included to help you with further research and/or implementation of the ideas found in this chapter.

Books

Tomi T Ahonen and Jim O'Reilly, *Digital Korea: Convergence of Broadband Internet, 3G Cell Phones, Multiplayer Gaming, Digital TV, Virtual Reality, Electronic Cash, Telematics, Robotics, E-Government and the Intelligent Home* (futuretext, 2007)

Chetan Sharma, Joe Herzog, and Victor Melfi, *Mobile Advertising: Supercharge Your Brand in the Exploding Wireless Market* (Wiley, 2008)

Magazines and Journals

MMA International Journal of Mobile Marketing, www.mmaglobal.com/modules/article/view.article.php/1420

Mobile Marketer, www.mobilemarketer.com

Mobile Marketing Magazine, www.mobilemarketingmagazine. co.uk

RCR Wireless News, www.rcrwireless.com

Marketing to Women

Lip-Sticking, www.lipsticking.com

The TrendSight Group, www.trendsight.com

Marketing to Hispanics

HispanSource, www.hispansource.org

Marketing to Millennials

Millennial Marketer, www.millennialmarketer.com

Marketing to Gen X

Reach X and Y, www.reachgroupconsulting.com

Marketing to Baby Boomers

Coming of Age, Incorporated, www.comingofage.com

Five Steps to Creating a Dynamic Mobile Marketing Campaign

Consumers use the mobile phone for a variety of reasons at different times of day. Most can be surmised through common sense. So any kind of marketing must be geared toward understanding the mindset during those gaps in the day.
—Mickey Alam Khan, Editor in Chief,
Mobile Marketer

Mobile marketing campaigns are lively and dynamic in ways that other marketing is not for a good reason: Your customer must actively engage in the marketing to get started. Once the campaign is underway, your business (through your marketing efforts) is in direct one-to-one contact with your customers. As an example, your text message coupon is sent to their phones, and when it arrives, it is likely to be read immediately, or your click-to-call button (a clickable link on a mobile web page that triggers a phone call) is handy when your customers need it, so they call you. Your mobile website might offer just the right mix of information that your customers can easily discover right in the palm of their hands.

But these dynamic campaigns do not magically appear without effort. Solid strategic planning must take place to make sure the campaign works the way you want it to work and achieves the direct customer connection. In this chapter, you will find the step-by-step process to strategize your mobile marketing campaign and determine the right tool(s) you'll need for the results you desire.

The Secret of Being Dynamic

The word "dynamic" is defined by Dictionary.com as:

1. *vigorous and purposeful,* full of energy, enthusiasm, and a sense of purpose, and able both to get things going and to get things done

2. *active and changing,* characterized by vigorous activity and producing or undergoing change and development

The definition of dynamic contains two components that are critical to our discussion of mobile marketing. First, mobile marketing is purposeful, and second, it is active. If you can create a campaign with a clearly defined purpose and make it active between you and your customers, then you have created a dynamic (and ultimately profitable) campaign.

In marketing, there are two ways to reach the consumer. One is to "push" marketing to them. Essentially, push marketing is actively reaching out to your target market without their permission or desire to receive your marketing messages. Push marketing can be introduced to people through the following ways:

- Interrupting TV shows or music on the radio with commercials

- Sending an unexpected brochure or sales letter in the mail

- Sending spam with computer-generated emails or phone-generated text messages

This type of marketing causes almost everyone to have a universal aversion to marketing and sales. No one wants to have messages or ads shoved at them when they are not interested.

The other way is to "pull" customers to you. Pull marketing creates content that your target market actually wants to receive. By giving it to them, you can market your company in the process. This type of marketing allows customers to forget where the marketing is coming from and just enjoy the value they receive. If pull marketing is done properly, customers actually want this content from you. All you need to do is purposefully and repeatedly put the content or offer in front of them. Pull marketing can be introduced in any of the following ways:

- Building an effective website and enticing your customers to visit it

- Creating a newsletter and encouraging customers to sign up for it

- Producing a video that shows viewers how to do something (if someone is interested in learning, they will look for these tutorials)

- Offering potential customers something of value such as a discount or valuable, timely information in exchange for permission to send a text message to them.

While it might seem surprising, both types of marketing work. Push marketing has worked for hundreds of years. If it didn't, companies would stop doing it. Your mailbox would not be filled with preapproved credit card offers if people didn't sign up for these offers in the first place. TV commercials would disappear if companies didn't find them profitable. Email spam would instantly stop appearing in your in-box if the products didn't sell.

However, push marketing is not working as well as it has in the past. In his book *Pyro Marketing*, Greg Stielstra discusses ways in which the effectiveness of push mass marketing has changed through the years:

> The era of mass marketing is ending. The promotion of a single product or service to everyone through an undifferentiated media reached its peak in the 1960s and its success convinced most marketers it was the only way. But the world has changed and mass tactics that worked so brilliantly thirty-five years before and which still seem perfectly sensible in the safety of the boardroom increasingly fail in the real, modern world. ... Yet many companies continue to use mass marketing, hoping it still wields its old influence.

He also explains how the change from three TV networks to hundreds is one example of how marketing as we knew it has completely changed. Although *Pyro Marketing* is well worth reading cover to cover, there is one important point that relates to mobile marketing: Mobile as a marketing tool requires a completely different mind-set when strategizing because the same old way of marketing will not work. Push marketing in the mobile arena is not acceptable because in spammed text messages, for example, it completely goes against best practices; in others, such as interrupting someone with a commercial message when they are trying to find something quickly, is just not practical. Pull marketing is the only effective way to market with mobile. To create an effective pull marketing campaign, start with a single question: "What's in it for the customers?" This brings us to the first of the five strategies involved in creating a dynamic mobile marketing campaign (Figure 2.1).

Five Steps to Creating a
Dynamic Mobile Marketing Campaign

❶ Figure out what your target market wants and offer it.
> Location-Specific Information
> Timely Knowledge
> Make Life Easier
> Financial Incentive
> Entertainment
> Connection

❷ Align what your target market wants with your desired outcome.
> Get New Customers
> Retain Current Customers
> Increase Purchases from Current Customers
> Brand Awareness

❸ Choose the right mobile marketing tool for this campaign.
> Voice
> Text Messaging
> Mobile Web
> Mobile Web Promotion:
>> Search
>> Advertising
>> Pay per Click
>> Publicity
> Social Networking
> Proximity Marketing

❹ Launch your mobile marketing campaign and market it.

❺ Track what is working and make any necessary adjustments.

Figure 2.1 If this book could be summed up in one page, this would be it: The Five Steps to Creating a Dynamic Mobile Marketing Campaign.

Step One: Figure Out What Your Target Market Wants and Offer It

There is almost nothing harder than trying to sell something that no one wants. The effort necessary to convince someone that they need what you are offering is unbelievably high and usually doesn't work. On the flip side, it is easy to sell something when people already want it. Think of a sidewalk vendor trying to sell hot chocolate in Phoenix in July. No matter how good the hot cocoa is or what kind of discount is offered, it is just not what people want to buy. Change the product to ice cold water, and the equation changes. Sales happen easily, and the customers are happy. You need to do the same thing with your mobile campaigns. Offer people something they already want, and your campaign will be substantially more successful and markedly easier to implement.

What's in It for Them?

Unlike other marketing tools, mobile only works if your customers have given you permission and outreach. Mobile is a pull-only marketing method. People are busy and overwhelmed with the huge number of marketing messages that reach them on a daily basis. With a mobile marketing campaign, you are asking people to add more marketing into their life. And, if you don't have a compelling reason for them to want to interact with you on mobile, they won't.

To start a pull marketing campaign, figure out what you can offer your customers that will add value to their day. Ask the questions/thought starters that are introduced later in this chapter at the end of Step One to determine your compelling reason for the interaction. Remember, people will only interact with marketing if there is something in it for them. If it seems like they are participating solely to receive advertising, your mobile campaign will not work. Make sure that you also offer value. To provide value, figure out how to combine what you have to offer with what your customers want. For instance, you can offer a coupon for a free movie, dessert, drink, or parking. By offering something customers want, you can entice them to ask for the offer on their mobile devices. Because it is a free sample of your product or service, you get what you want because customers will typically buy more from you than just the free item. Let's start with what they want.

Six Ways to Provide Value with Mobile

Since you have to improve your customers' lives in some way for them to accept mobile marketing from you, here are six options for providing value via mobile that will enhance their lives sufficiently for them to engage with your campaign.

1. Location-Specific Information

This category is a no-brainer for providing information to your customers via mobile. Location-specific knowledge is the No. 1 reason that people access the mobile web for mobile search. It is the most likely reason for someone to call to find out where your business is in relation to where they are. Regardless of whatever fun, creative, and exciting elements you include in your mobile campaign, always include location-specific information in your mobile presence. A location-focused campaign includes addresses, driving directions, maps, photos of your storefront, and anything else that will help someone find you physically or in relation to your location. Make sure you have keywords included in your local search campaign. For example, if you are a plumber, be sure to put keywords that people would search for to find you (plumber, plumbing, frozen pipes, and plugged toilet) in your wording on your mobile site. Then use these same words when you are asked for tags or keywords to describe your site at any point. Be sure you have your business listed in every local search engine/local directory possible. (Check the Mobile Search Resource section at the end of Chapter 10 for a complete action checklist.)

2. Timely Knowledge

If you need to alert your target market quickly about special information, even when an email might be too slow, mobile is the perfect way to provide value to your customers. One example could be a pricing alert (gas prices are going up in four hours), an availability alert (your favorite hair stylist has an opening in three hours, or the hard-to-find item you have been waiting for is now in stock), or a combination of these (we have open tables tonight, and if you come in before 7 PM, you can receive a free dessert). This could also be a readiness alert (when your order is ready to be picked up) because once you check your email at home or retrieve your phone messages, you don't want to go out again. Travel alerts are a perfect example of timely knowledge. If a flight is delayed or the gate has changed, this information is instantly valuable wherever you are.

3. Make Life Easier

Anything you can offer that makes life convenient and more efficient for your customers is a good option for your mobile campaign. This category is wide open because there are dozens of ways to make your customers' lives easier via mobile. A good place to start when brainstorming this value proposition is to consider what questions your customers/potential customers ask you frequently. Think about where your customers are and what information they might find helpful to access now. For example, a busy working mom needs menu choices for dinner tonight when she's in the grocery store, or she needs a list of healthy snack options for her child's classroom. Or consider the exercise enthusiast who tracks workouts and calorie consumption and wants instant access to this data anytime, anywhere. Developing a clear picture of your customers helps in answering the following questions: Who are they? What do they do with their lives? What problems do they want you to solve? How can interacting with your business make their lives better, and how does that extend to mobile?

4. Financial Incentive

People love to save money, find a good deal, and feel special. Finding a way to do that for your customers provides value. When you offer coupons, discounts, or special offers via mobile, be creative. Integrate your offer into your customers' mobile environment so when they first receive it, the offer is actually there when they want to use it. One example is using signs outside your business to offer a text message coupon that can be redeemed instantly by walking inside the store. Incorporating your loyalty program tracking (offers to buy 10 items and get the 11th one free) into your mobile campaign not only gives your customers a reason to interact with you via mobile, it also keeps them buying directly from you. Keep in mind that customers will want a more intrusive, customized coupon (one they receive on their phones) to offer a bigger incentive. A coupon for a 50-cent discount that they see in the newspaper may be enough to motivate them to get out the scissors, clip the coupon, and take it with them to the grocery store, but they need more incentive to receive something on their mobile device. They might want to get a combination of coupons or a bigger ticket item. Just be careful not to overdo this option. Because a financial incentive is easy, it is likely to be the most used and the first to be overused.

5. Entertainment

Anyone who has a few minutes to spare and a mobile device is a likely candidate for you to entertain via mobile. Games, trivia, contests, recordings, and scavenger hunts are good mobile options. You can create your own games, sponsor an existing one, or even offer people a list of game sites. If customers have to sit and wait for you at any point, your waiting area can become one of your best marketing tools or a place where people don't mind waiting. Or what if people in a waiting room somewhere else, standing in line, riding the bus/subway, or just hanging out with nothing to do began interacting with your business? Think about ways you can entertain your customers via mobile that also provide value to them.

6. Connection

Younger generations have grown up connected to each other through the Internet and cell phones in ways that many other generations have not. This generation is connected by mobile phones unlike no other generation. Through text messaging and sites such as MySpace and Facebook, these under-30 folks now expect to reach out to their network of friends at any time through their mobile devices. The tools that allow them to do this are some form of social networking software. Don't be tempted to dismiss mobile social networking just because you may not personally understand it. There are ways to add connection to the lives of your customers, even if they are not the younger crowd. One example of this is OrbitzTLC Traveler Update feature (www.Orbitz.com/App/ViewTravel WatchHome). Through this mobile social networking site, travelers can update and check timely information including parking information, security delays, taxi lines, and other comments from fellow travelers via their mobile devices. OrbitzTLC connects people who are otherwise strangers as they are traveling to and from the same place or within the same airport. This service connects them in ways that add value to their lives and gives them this connection via their mobile device.

These connections can be offered as a value through sponsorship of a social networking site, advertising on one, or creating one for your customers to use. This will work best if your customers want to start a group offline naturally or if they discover a common interest while they are interacting with your business. This connection also links customers to your business. The "popularity" of your company or anyone in your company can attract customers who want to be connected to you. Having a solid brand community comes in handy when a company is providing value through connections.

Only One in Four Receptive to "Mobile Marketing"

According to a U.S. Mobile Marketing Association (MMA) Annual Attitude & Usage study from 2007, only one in four respondents indicated they were receptive to receiving mobile marketing. However, this statistic doesn't alarm me. Of course, most people don't want to be on the receiving end of marketing campaigns; no one likes to think they are being sold something.

It conjures up images of the snake oil salesmen of days gone by. But people actually like adding value to their lives, and when they find something that enhances their lives, they are willing to engage with it. When customers find something worthwhile, they do not refer to it as marketing in their own minds. Instead, it is helpful/fun/entertaining to them, but it still is "marketing" to you. Take the Redbox Free Movie Monday text message campaign (www.redbox.com/Help/Signup.aspx), for example. Customers can sign up to get a text message coupon each Monday for a free movie rental. As one of these customers, I can verify that when the text message arrives each Monday, I think, "There's my free movie." I'm not even giving it a thought that Redbox is "marketing" to me. So, if the question in the MMA survey said, "Are you open to receiving text message offers for free stuff from companies you trust?" I'm certain the respondents would have been much more open to that.

What Is Your Compelling Reason for Mobile Interaction?

Knowing what your customers want is only part of the equation. You need to know what compelling offers you will be providing to them. Use the following list of questions to spark your creativity in thinking about what your customers want:

- What information do your customers need from you and need right now?

- What are the most common questions your customers ask?

- Are there any tidbits of knowledge about your products, services, or business history your customers would find interesting or helpful?

- What would your customers like to win (prizes from your product line, services you offer, or special opportunities)?

- Are there topics on which your customers could offer their opinions or insights?

- Could you make a list of what your customers can photograph and send to you or upload to a website for a group of all your customers to see? (This can be a photo contest featuring your products or services.)

- Do you sell anything they want to buy quickly or impulsively?

- Can you compile a list of interesting trivia questions and answers about your company, branded product, or service?

- What happens in your day-to-day operations to which your customers need alerts?

- What kinds of coupons would be useful to your customers?

- Do you sponsor any events that your customers attend?

- Does your company sell any products for which a video tutorial would be useful?

- Do you exhibit at any trade shows?

- What fundraising efforts do you do?

- Where can customers/potential customers see you or your product? An event? Workshop? Seminar?

- What new product or service do you have that your customers can be the first to know about, buy, use, or experience?

Keep the answers to these questions handy as you design your mobile marketing campaign. When you start the technology part of the campaign, this information will be helpful when you focus on what it is you want to offer your customers. Stay focused on what your customers want and what you can provide to enhance their lives. When you can add value to your customers' lives with mobile, you will have succeeded in the first step of a dynamic mobile marketing campaign.

Step Two: Align What Your Target Market Wants with Your Desired Outcome

A clearly defined outcome is essential to determining the ROI (return on investment) for any marketing campaign. It is especially important when a new technology is in place because it may be tempting to just try something to see what happens. But without an initial goal set firmly in place, it will be impossible to know whether the strategy worked.

Determine the Outcome You Want

The next step in a dynamic mobile marketing campaign is to align what the customer wants with what you want. With a mobile campaign, as with any marketing initiative, you want to define the outcome in advance. Be specific. What exactly do you want your customers to do after they interact with you on mobile? What problem does your company need to resolve by this particular marketing effort? Ultimately, the following four objective outcomes are essential in any successful marketing effort:

1. Acquisition of new customers

2. Increased sales to current customers

3. Retention of current customers

4. Brand awareness

The most desired marketing outcome by a business is the acquisition of new customers. Most ads are aimed at that outcome, and that is what most businesses design their marketing to accomplish. However, it is often easier to increase sales from current customers and keep current customers happy than it is to keep trying to attract new customers. Since mobile is such an interactive tool combined with other marketing efforts, it is also easier to implement mobile campaigns aimed at current customers. So as you consider your marketing objectives, begin your initial focus on the second item on the list: increased sales to current customers. Then focus on retaining current customers, and then move back to the more attractive goal of acquiring new customers. If you have a marketing objective to follow and must achieve it regardless of its ease or common sense, don't worry. The reality is that you can achieve any marketing outcome with mobile marketing as long as you provide solid value to a reasonably mobile-savvy target audience and market your mobile campaign effectively.

Increased Sales to Current Customers

The reason it is easy to increase sales to current customers is that they are the ones who are already buying from you. They are already in your place of business, they receive your other marketing pieces, and they trust you. Current customers are most likely to believe that you will treat them right via mobile because you already treat them right with their other business. So as you strategize the outcome you want, look to mobile for ways to increase sales from this prime market. Think about what your customers purchase from you already that you can alert them to buy more of, schedule their next appointment, or otherwise interact with you again. Look at how you can make their lives easier with a mobile alert. If you don't know what that is, ask them. Remember to offer a financial incentive to current customers as well as new ones. Don't be a company that only offers the best rates to new customers and disregards its loyal customers. This just makes people resent your business and want to be a new customer somewhere else.

Retention of Current Customers

Retaining customers is all about providing good customer service, and you can accomplish quite a lot via mobile. Mobile-enabled customer service does not have to be complicated; you don't have to launch a complete mobile customer relationship management system. It can be as simple as offering mobile reminders, being available to customers via text messaging for communication or ordering, giving them a way to submit feedback to you when they are mobile, or entertaining them at times when they are waiting for you. Anything you can provide via mobile that gives more value to your customers will help retain them.

Acquisition of New Customers

The Holy Grail of marketing—getting new customers—is certainly an achievable task. Although it requires a bit more on the marketing side because these new people are not already in your circle of influence, the payoff is exciting. You can effectively drive new customers to your business through mobile coupons, any mobile web promotion strategies (search, advertising, pay-per-click [an online ad model where an advertiser pays for the ad only when a customer clicks on it and into the advertiser's site], or publicity), or even location-based marketing. Text messaging and the mobile web, especially when providing location-specific information, are good tools to use to get new customers. Remember, when you are attracting new customers, you need to build trust through your marketing, particularly when you are asking them to give you personal information such as their cell phone numbers.

Brand Awareness

Creating brand awareness helps with all three of these more trackable goals: the acquisition of new customers, increased sales to current customers, and retention of current customers. A new customer will be more willing to purchase a known brand. Customers are always reassured by seeing the brand they buy being marketed. Everyone likes to be on a winning team and be part of something successful, which is accomplished by seeing the brand marketed. If brand awareness is linked to a customer simply seeing your ad, logo, or company name but not necessarily by taking any additional action, then brand awareness on its own should not ever be the only goal for a mobile marketing campaign. It is just too easy to add the next step on to any campaign and get a quantifiable response from your customer, such as getting someone to click through to a landing from an ad, make a phone call, or opt in to a text message responder. To have a mobile ad that goes nowhere or requires no response of any kind is a waste of advertising dollars. Brand awareness should be only part of your stated outcome and never all of it with mobile. That said, mobile advertising is a great brand awareness tool to use as part of your overall campaign. Social networking can also work as an effective brand awareness tool if you do it right.

There's one other note about branding. Branding is all about the brand and not the customer. How does knowing and/or recognizing a brand help or add value to the life of the customer? It doesn't. Brand awareness is not a customer-focused marketing outcome, and that is precisely why I am not a big fan of brand awareness for the sake of it alone.

Step Three: Choose the Right Mobile Marketing Tool for This Campaign

When you're ready to choose the right tool to use in your campaign, look for one that is likely to provide value to your customers and to accomplish your desired outcome. In subsequent chapters, I will cover how to implement each of the following specific marketing tools: voice, text messaging, mobile websites, mobile promotion strategies, social networking, and proximity marketing. But for now, let's focus on which ones to choose that will accomplish your two-pronged goal of providing value to the customer and staying focused. It is important to keep the process of choosing your tool separate from learning how to use it. It just becomes too complicated to cover the details of how to use a particular method and why it was selected at the same time.

So let's take a closer look at each of the mobile marketing tools that are covered in Part 2 and how they can provide value in each of the six ways discussed earlier. This is important because you can choose the right tool knowing that you will be providing one of the core six values to customers, and you can determine which marketing tool to use depending upon the value you are trying to provide. (Returning to the section "Six Ways to Provide Value with Mobile" earlier in the chapter will be helpful after you read about each of the mobile tactics.) If a particular tool provides a specific value that is aligned more closely with one of the outcomes, it will be noted. You'll see that several items are marked with asterisks; these are the best tools to provide the specific value listed.

Smart Mobile Marketing Matrix

The Smart Mobile Marketing Matrix (Figure 2.2) can be used to figure out what value you are going to provide to your customers and how it will align with the objectives you have. So you might start by going across the top row and highlighting which of the values you are going to provide to your customers with mobile. Then decide what outcome you are seeking, including new customers, new business from current ones, customer retention, or brand awareness. Then take a look at the information that follows about which mobile marketing tools are the best match for what you want to achieve. Use the Smart Mobile Marketing Matrix to help you start your campaign strategy off on the right foot. After all, the first step of your campaign is taking into account what your customers want. The matrix is a good tactical reminder to put your customers' needs first. As an example, let's say you want to increase purchases from your current customers, and you have an idea that they might like to know when you have an open appointment unexpectedly. You would write "Open Appointment Reminders" in the row Increase Purchases and the column Timely Knowledge. Then you could proceed with the rest of the chart to see what else you can offer that would be of value to your customers.

Smart Mobile Marketing Matrix

WHAT DOES YOUR CUSTOMER WANT?

The idea with the matrix is to match up what you want with what your customer wants. Fill in a square with the type of mobile marketing tool you will be using for your campaign.

WHAT DO YOU WANT?	Location-Specific Information	Timely Knowledge	Make Their Life Easier	Financial Incentive	Entertainment	Connection
Retain Customers						
Increase Purchases						
New Customers						
Brand Awareness						

Figure 2.2   The Smart Mobile Marketing Matrix is designed to help you decide what your goals are and how they align with your customers' desires.

Voice

Voice is the most logical way of connecting and communicating your ideas and company over a mobile phone. Basically, your customer is using a device whose original purpose is making phone calls to find and/or engage with your business by making a phone call.

Location-Specific Information	When your customers need to find you, talking to you can be the best option for them. Voice can be a great match for some pieces of location-specific information. If you have a particularly difficult-to-find location, you can post a sign that gives a number to call for a recorded message about how to find you. You can put the sign at the spot where people often get lost trying to find you.
Timely Knowledge	The best way to offer outbound timely knowledge via voice on mobile is to use an outbound calling service and get customers to agree to be called when there is timely information they need to know. You will need to have something timely and trusted by your customers so they agree to be called on their mobile by a phone service, but if you have the right mix of what people want and that built-in trust, this can work well.
Make Life Easier	Offering recordings for your customers can make their lives easier. These recordings can be informational, topical news, or even announcements about upcoming events. Anytime you can make contacting you easier for customers, you ultimately make their lives easier.
Financial Incentive	Offering a discount or special directly via voice is problematic because of the trouble redeeming a verbal offer. You could use a recorded message to suggest people opt in to a text message mobile coupon.
Entertainment	Again, a recorded message is the most likely option to offer entertainment via voice.
**** Connection	This is the best match for voice as a mobile marketing tool. Voice connects your customers with you via the good old fashioned way of calling you directly.

Text Messaging

If you are ready to start a mobile campaign or are just learning where to begin, choose text messaging. It is the most common use of mobile devices (besides calling), and more and more people launch text message campaigns every day. Text messaging is the "now" marketing tool of mobile.

Location-Specific Information	To provide location-specific info via text message, be sure you are listed in Google's Local Business Center. You can get a free listing (www.google.com/local/add/businessCenter). When people use the Google SMS service, your business may be displayed.
**** Timely Knowledge	Text messaging seems like it was built for communicating timely knowledge. If you have anything that your customers need to know from you in a timely manner, text messaging is the best way to go.
Make Life Easier	It is possible to make life easier via text message. Think about what tidbits of knowledge your customers would like to receive from you that will enhance their life. This is an effective customer retention tool because you can keep the lines of communication open between you and your customers.
**** Financial Incentive	Providing mobile text coupons is an ideal way to provide financial incentive. Implemented properly, this can be a staple tool for your campaigns.
Entertainment	You can certainly entertain people with text messages by asking trivia questions, offering jokes, or providing other fun tidbits of information. Often called text clubs, subscription text messages can be an excellent marketing tool.
Connection	If you are offering connection with your business, your brand, or your key personnel via texting, you are one of the few, the proud, and the brave. You also may be smart, too, especially if you have customers who prefer texting to communicate.

Mobile Web

Consumers expect virtually every business to have a web presence these days, and it won't take long before they feel the same way about the mobile web. People want to find whatever they want to know at any time. So if they go onto the mobile web, you want them to find you and your business.

**** Location-Specific Information	This is the perfect application for the mobile web. Local mobile search delivers visitors to a mobile web presence that gives them everything they need to know from wherever they are.
Timely Knowledge	Timely information is not best passed along via the mobile web. Certainly it is OK to list timely information on your site, but don't expect that people will seek it out or remember to interact with your mobile site in the right time frame.
**** Make Life Easier	Making life easier for your customers is the perfect use of the mobile web, and there are many ways to do this. Remember to keep it simple with bullet points, 1-2-3 Steps/Keys, and so forth, so your visitor can read it quickly for whatever they need. One example of this is mobile Allrecipes.com, which gives mobile grocery shoppers a way to quickly and easily search for recipes by ingredient.
Financial Incentive	Providing financial incentive to your customers on the mobile web can be effective, but it probably is not the best use of the tool. Your financial offer would need to be tied to a text message coupon or another way for your customer to be alerted to your offer.
Entertainment	Entertainment is good to provide via the mobile web. Almost anything you can create—from content to games to productivity applications to photos—can be delivered via the mobile web.
Connection	Connecting with your customers via the mobile web is all about content and social networking. Any time people are visiting your mobile site, they are connecting with your business. Give them a reason to do it and make it easy, and this can be a great tool for providing connection.

Mobile Search

Mobile search puts your mobile website within reach of your customers so they can find you when they are looking for your company or what you offer. Much like desktop search optimization (doing what you can to be listed closest to the top of the results on a search engine), mobile search is important to your marketing.

**** Location-Specific Information	Mobile search is the best tool to provide location-specific information. In addition to having your own mobile site, you can list your business on local directory sites. This really helps when your customers go directly to these sources and then search. Being available on mobile search is the perfect way to provide location-specific information to your target audience.
Timely Knowledge	A person searching on mobile is seeking to find something in a timely fashion. The better you do with mobile search engine optimization (SEO) strategies, the more likely you are to provide your customer with timely knowledge.
Make Life Easier	Making your customers' lives easier and providing timely knowledge via mobile search is much the same. Just do what you need to do to be found when your customers need you.
Financial Incentive	It is hard to provide financial incentive through mobile search.
Entertainment	If you have a portion of your mobile site that is entertaining, you could work to get it listed in mobile search engines and directories in the entertainment category or under that keyword.
Connection	Any time your customers want to connect with you and can easily find you, that's connection.

Mobile Advertising

Mobile advertising, placing either graphic banner ads or text ads on mobile websites other than your own, is an excellent mobile marketing tool. It is easy to think of mobile advertising as the perfect tool for brand awareness because it is that and so much more. Be sure to add the next step of direct response to your mobile advertising campaigns.

**** Location-Specific Information	By directing your mobile ad to click through to a store locator page or your direction page, you can add all the location-specific information that your customers will need.
Timely Knowledge	Your mobile ad can click through to your mobile website, a landing page, or even a click-to-call page. Depending upon what your customers are likely to be looking for when they come across your ad, you can make sure they get to the right and most timely information.
Make Life Easier	If your ads are served on relevant sites, it is likely that you can make your customers' lives easier because your ad will seem more like content than advertising. Also, if your customers are looking for what you offer and your ad helps them find it, you have made life easier for them.
**** Financial Incentive	Mobile advertising is a great tool to share financial incentive. Your ads can click through to coupons or fill-in forms that will send out rewards, incentives, or special offers.
Entertainment	Using the click-to-video option is your best bet for entertaining your customer. Use this method in the same way you would use YouTube for marketing.
Connection	Most people do not feel highly connected to other people or to brands through advertising, so this is not the best tool to use when you are trying to provide connection as a value.

Mobile Publicity

In mobile publicity, your target audience is the media: journalists, reporters, bloggers, and producers who are looking for an expert or a source of information for a current assignment with a fast approaching deadline. If they are searching for sources via mobile, it is likely a breaking story or very timely, or otherwise they would do the search from their desktop computer.

Location-Specific Information	You won't be trying to provide location-specific information to the media through your mobile publicity campaign. However, if the story for which you are an expert is tied to a specific location, be sure to include the location as part of your mobile search strategy.
**** Timely Knowledge	When the media needs a contact, they need it now, especially if they are searching for a source via mobile. By having a mobile PR campaign in place, you help them get their answer fast.
**** Make Life Easier	Making life easier for the media is the basic premise of getting media coverage for your business. Having a mobile friendly media kit and making the kit easy to find are the two key components to this strategy.
Financial Incentive	Not applicable.
Entertainment	Not applicable.
Connection	Getting the media connected with the person they need to interview to complete their assignment is why you launch a mobile publicity campaign.

Social Networking

Social networking is all about people connecting with other people. Keep this in mind when deciding what to do to facilitate or participate in social networking. Also, as you will learn in Chapter 11, social networking will likely be a tool for marketing your mobile campaign.

Location-Specific Information	With the exception of the mobile social networking communities that are specifically designed around location (like Brightkite and Socialight), this is not what you would use social networking to accomplish.
Timely Knowledge	When done at events, social networking is a perfect use of mobile as a timely tool. Everyone attending a particular event and networking socially via mobile will appreciate the timeliness of the tool. In daily life, it is not as likely that this will be a good match for the value unless your target audience is college students.
Make Life Easier	It is really up to people doing the networking to decide to set it up to make their lives easier, so you don't really have to try to prove this value to your customers.
Financial Incentive	You can certainly set up a financial incentive via microblogging (i.e., Twitter), and it can work nicely. Consider this a decent match of the tool to the value.
**** Entertainment	If you have participated in social networking, you know it is entertaining. If you can include your business in the networking in an entertaining fashion, this can work well.
**** Connection	Social networking is all about connection, so this tool is perfect for providing this value. The trick is figuring out how to use mobile social networking for marketing while not going too commercial and pushing away potential customers.

Proximity Marketing

Any time you are marketing to someone specifically because they are in your proximity, you are involved in proximity marketing. This could be a Bluetooth campaign (people with Bluetooth devices are invited to accept a multimedia message to their devices or are reminded to check into their location-specific mobile network).

**** Location-Specific Information	This is a bit of a no-brainer: By definition, location-based marketing offers information that is location specific. So of course this type of tool is perfect for the job.
Timely Knowledge	Depending upon the service that you are using and how you're using it, a location-based marketing service will be timely. If your customers are signed up for a Brightkite-type service and getting texts every time one of their friends moves around, it can provide timely info. If you are soliciting mobile reviews that will be available at any time, it does not.
Make Life Easier	By using some of the more advanced features that location-based marketing will be able to accomplish in the future, it may make people's lives easier. If it is done incorrectly, it can be as annoying as email spam, which certainly makes life easier for no one.
Financial Incentive	You can have a coupon or special offer that is location specific. Anyone who is engaged with the location-based service would see it. Through Bluetooth technology, financial incentives can be offered to anyone in the area who chooses to participate. This is a great use of offering something of value to someone based on where they are located.
Entertainment	It is entertaining for people to engage with mobile as it relates to their location. If you can tap into this and find a way to include your business in the entertainment, it can work for you.
Connection	People using location-based services may be connected with others who are doing the same. You may be able to work this value into the tool.

Step Four: Launch Your Mobile Marketing Campaign and Market It

I won't go into a detailed explanation here about how to implement your mobile marketing campaign because that is the complete focus of Chapter 4. The one point that cannot be emphasized enough is that now is the time to start your mobile marketing campaign. Mobile marketing will only be the new frontier for a short while; the landscape will become crowded quickly. It will be better to launch a viable campaign now than a perfect campaign later. So start now. The marketing of your mobile campaign is covered in Chapter 5. Be aware that marketing your campaign is critical to the success of your mobile efforts. If you don't let your customers know you are doing anything with mobile, they are not likely to participate.

Step Five: Track What Is Working and Make Any Necessary Adjustments

> *Half the money I spend on advertising is wasted; the trouble is I don't know which half.*
>
> —John Wanamaker (1838–1922)

This adage about advertising simply does not have to be true. When Wanamaker said it at the turn of the last century, it probably was true since he was considered "the father of modern advertising." But it is possible that the concept and the ability to track advertising's success or failure didn't exist then. In the 21st century, we can track what marketing works and what doesn't. This is especially true when advertising on the Internet and via mobile.

In my early marketing days, I worked with the people in my company whose job it was to interact with the customers to track our campaigns. The same holds true with you. You can't launch an effective mobile coupon campaign if the salespeople don't know how to accept coupons and track them properly. Training your personnel will be essential. Using new analytics software for your mobile web will help you track your marketing details right to the sale to prove your ROI. More specific details about the ways to track your mobile marketing campaign will be covered in Chapter 6.

Chapter Updates and Online Resource Guide

Updates to this chapter and its related Online Resource Guide are available at www.mobilemarketinghandbook.com/Updates/Five Steps.

The Online Resource Guide for Chapter 2 includes links for all sites listed in this chapter.

Legal Issues and Implications of Mobile Marketing

Unfair or deceptive acts or practices in or affecting commerce, are hereby declared unlawful.
—Section 5 of FTC Act (15 USC § 45)

Author's Note: The information in this chapter is neither legal advice nor a comprehensive list of all laws governing mobile marketing. Rather, it is a set of guidelines to point out legal implications of mobile marketing. Consult your own attorney for specific legal advice as you proceed with your own campaigns.

Why Legal Issues Are Strategic Issues

While it is important to stay within legal guidelines in all marketing campaigns, it is even more important in the mobile arena because of the intimate relationship between cell phones and the people who use them. No one wants to have unsolicited marketing messages interrupting them on their mobile devices. After all, these devices are with them all day and night, at work, at home, on vacation, and anywhere they are. Cell phone companies are particularly sensitive to users who will contact their customer service departments with any complaints when they feel annoyed or harassed. Before you launch your mobile marketing campaigns, make sure your plans are within legal limits.

Best Practices Are Not Optional

In many ways, mobile marketing is a new frontier, but it isn't the lawless Wild West. The carriers are often the enforcement arm of industry best practices, and they will shut down short codes for non-compliance to best practices and approve all campaigns that go through their networks. Laws already clearly cover what can and cannot be done in mobile marketing. It's no surprise that the rules the Federal Trade Commission (FTC) has set forth for advertising also apply to the mobile environment. Additional laws cover mobile marketing specifically as well. Let's go over a few of the concepts.

First, the broadest law governing advertising in the U.S. and Canada covers the concept of being fair and truthful. The bottom line is: Don't be deceptive, unfair, misleading, or false. If your mobile marketing campaign misrepresents the facts or omits crucial information that a consumer needs before making an informed decision about your company, then it is considered deceptive. If your campaign could cause your customers any substantial injury that they cannot reasonably avoid, then it is considered unfair. As the lowest common denominator, if you wouldn't want to include your mother in the advertising campaign, then it is likely to be deceptive or unfair. Just don't do it.

Consider the following ways to stay on track:

- Copyright – Don't violate a copyright that protects an author's rights in "original works of authorship." Unless you are 100 percent certain a work is not under copyright, don't use it.

- Trademark – Watch for violations of company trademarks. Their words, logos, and trademark images are not available for your use.

- Rights of Publicity and Privacy – Don't use a person (celebrity or otherwise) to promote your company without that person's permission. Everyone's persona is protected from use for commercial gain by unauthorized parties.

- Contractual Rights/Implied – Look for any other contracts (written or implied) that you could be violating.

- Free – When using the word "free," be clear about what is free and be honest about any conditions that need to be met.

- Headlines – Write truthful headlines. Though it is tempting to use outrageous claims in a headline and tell the truth later, people may make a decision based on the deceptive information in the headline and not bother to read the rest.

- Fine Print – Don't hide anything in fine print. Tell your potential customers exactly what they will be receiving. People have a right to know what they have signed up for, and you are legally obligated to tell them.

Mobile Messaging Meets the Law

While there are many practical and smart marketing reasons why you should never send unsolicited messages to people's phones, the U.S. CAN-SPAM Act of 2003 is one major reason. This is the law that applies to email and to commercial text messages as well. Of course, buying lists of mobile phone numbers and sending text messages to these numbers is against the law. Even when you send messages that your customers have requested, you need to stay within the guidelines of the law. But there are a couple of important requirements that apply specifically to mobile messaging. While email is an opt-out process (meaning you must offer a way for customers to opt out of receiving your email messages), mobile messaging is an opt-in and an opt-out process. You are legally required to get "express prior authorization" before sending any commercial message to a mobile device, and you must also offer a way for customers to stop receiving messages.

You may obtain express prior authorization orally or in writing, but it cannot be a negative option (i.e., I will send this to you unless you tell me not to do so). When people send a message from their mobile devices, they are opting in. You can safely send them text messages in reply to their requests and other messages specifically related to the campaign they originally requested, but nothing else. For example, suppose you have a Two-for-One Taco Deal and 100 people send you a text message asking for that coupon. That coupon is all you can send if you specifically stated in your marketing materials that the request was for a Two-for-One Taco Deal. But if you stated in your marketing that they were signing up for the Weekly Special including this week's special is the Two-for-One Taco Deal, then next week you can send them the 10-percent-discount-on-burritos offer. So word your campaigns carefully. Market what you really want to send.

If you are working on a premium short message service (SMS) campaign where your customers will be charged for sending or receiving messages (beyond their normal text message rates from their carrier), you must offer a double opt-in. This means the customers must send a text to request participation in your premium campaign. Then, you must text them back and ask them to verify that they want to send/get the next text message for which they will actually be charged. You can send the premium message only after customers reply a second time (that's why the phrase "double opt-in" is used) to verify that they understand they will be charged for the next message.

Mobile Marketing Association Best Practices

The best resource to use for your mobile messaging campaigns is the Mobile Marketing Association Consumer Best Practices Guidelines (www.mmaglobal.com/bestpractices. pdf). This free document outlines everything you need to consider when launching your messaging campaign. It will help you build your campaign on solid ground during the planning and strategy phase. It is also likely to comply with international laws regarding mobile marketing. The association updates the Best Practices often to keep track of existing laws in the industry.

When your customers agree to receive mobile messages from you, you must identify your business name, let them know they may be charged for receiving these messages, and assure them that they can revoke consent at any time. You also have to provide a method for opting out of your messages. One way to do this is to tell them the opt-out word to use to stop receiving messages from you. Usually, the word is "Stop" or "Remove." If they send you a text with that word to any message you send them, your software should automatically remove them from the subscription list.

And the Lucky Winner Is ...

Anytime you want to launch a sweepstakes-like promotion, be careful that your promotion does not become an illegal lottery or a form of gambling. Although this isn't specific legal advice, consider the following formula as what constitutes an illegal lottery: Prize + Chance + Consideration. Simply, when you offer a prize that is won by chance by someone who paid for this chance with time or money (consideration), then you have created a lottery. Creating a lottery is illegal.

Generally, you can prevent your promotion from becoming a lottery by taking an element out of the equation. For example, if there is no prize, there is no lottery. (Not offering a prize usually eliminates all participants, so it's best not to eliminate that one.) But you can eliminate chance by making it a skills-based competition, such as having participants answer a question. Most often, the consideration factor is eliminated when people expend time or money. If you are charging participants a fee to enter, then offer an alternate entry form that is free. This is where that magical phrase "No purchase necessary" originated. Usually, the option of eliminating consideration will be enough to protect you. However, proceed with caution even when using that option because certain states have different laws. My best advice is to get professional legal advice before proceeding with any sweepstakes. It's tricky, and the consequences can be sizable.

What Your Users Generate and How It Affects You

The days when a company completely controlled all the content on its website are long gone, or at least they should be. Smart marketers know that having users participate on websites via blogs, comments, forums, or social networking builds a dynamic presence. This is also being carried over into the mobile Internet. Two U.S. laws will have an impact in this area: the Digital Millennium Copyright Act (DMCA) and the Communications Decency Act (CDA), both of which cover publisher immunity for third-party content. Basically, these laws specify that you are not liable for content that other people add to your website. However, there are certain protections you must enforce.

You must have procedures in place that allow other companies and individuals to protect their copyright. If a user on your site submits content that infringes on someone else's copyright, you need to provide a way to protect the original copyright owner. Usually this means taking the content in question off the site. But you are not obligated to take any action whatsoever for trademark infringements, defamation, or obscenity that is created by third-party users on your site. Of course, you can have your own policies regarding these points, but you are not legally obligated to do so. The bottom line here is to have clear-cut procedures to follow.

The Under-13 Crowd

If you market to children under 13 or believe that kids under that age are likely to provide personal information to participate in your mobile site, be sure to contact an attorney for professional guidance. The U.S. Children's Online Privacy Protection Act applies to all operators of website and online services (including mobile) that intend to reach children under 13 or have actual knowledge (regardless of whether the age group is targeted) that children under the age of 13 visit their websites. There is a complex set of laws that include posting a privacy policy, obtaining "verifiable parental consent," advising parents/legal guardians that they can review the child's personal information, and establishing and maintaining reasonable security procedures.

May I See Your ID, Please?

If you offer adult content (anything that should only be available to adults, including dating sites, erotica, violent games, grown-up social networking, or gambling), make sure you have a solid age verification system. Remember two key points: Make sure you don't collect data from anyone who doesn't match your age requirements, and don't allow a back-button function to work if someone admits he or she is too young, and then tries to put in an older age. If users can't prove they are adults, you can't send adult content to them.

Privacy, Sweet Privacy

The issue of privacy in mobile marketing will likely become a hot topic. Mobile devices tie personal information to mobile searches, location, and contacts in a way that no other media really does. Your newspaper doesn't track where you are reading it, whether you are at home, on the bus, or at the neighborhood coffee shop. Your TV doesn't know which family member is watching, much in the same way as your computer doesn't know who made which search inquiry. Since most people don't share a cell phone (even with their spouses), anything that a person does with his or her cell phone is usually traceable to that person. This data is highly personal. And while it may be helpful as a marketing tool (mobile search engine algorithms incorporate past search data into results to display for a particular mobile device), it is also alarming if you consider the implications of this data being acquired or demanded.

Joyce Meskis, the owner of Denver's famous Tattered Cover Book Store, fought all the way to the Colorado Supreme Court to keep local authorities from obtaining a book title purchased by a suspect in a drug case. According to the court, the book buyer's purchases could remain anonymous according to his First Amendment rights. It may not be long before a person's mobile records are subpoenaed or used inappropriately, and someone has to fight for privacy. The ideals of privacy advocates and mobile marketers are likely to clash, and the outcome will be significant. Consumers will probably advocate for more privacy rights and be rewarded for their efforts. It is just too easy for fairly personal data to be compiled by cell phone carriers and others that may leave the consumer vulnerable.

What you need to know now about privacy and your legal obligations is simple: You must have a privacy policy if you collect personally identifiable information. This is established in the FTC's Fair Information Practice Principles. This policy includes Notice (telling your customers what your policy is), Choice (a way for them to choose how their information is shared), Access (clear explanation of who has access to their data), Security (what measures you will follow to ensure their data is safe), and Enforcement (what you will do to enforce your policies). Writing a privacy policy is not for the faint hearted or for those who don't want to waste time or do it wrong. Use a template for privacy policy or hire legal counsel to write one for you. Then stick to it.

When you are contemplating a privacy policy, consider the consumer. The more privacy you can offer to the consumer, the better. First, if the laws become more restrictive than they were when you launched your policy and you have a consumer-friendly policy, you will have fewer changes to make in your business model. Additionally, there is the potential for making customers feel as though you are Big Brother looking over their shoulders through technology. It may not be well received. Use the technology to benefit the consumer, and keep their privacy in mind at the same time.

Location-Based Legal Requirements

While there is no legislation in the U.S. that specifically covers location-based services (Bluetooth in particular), carriers and prudent marketers are treading softly. In the U.K., where mobile marketing is more active, some legislation initially restricted Bluetooth outreach, but then the legislation was rescinded. However, the Mobile Marketing Association (MMA) and the Direct Marketing Association (a U.K. association) are suggesting that mobile marketers follow the same regime of getting permission from consumers before contacting them, even if a law does not require it.

Consequences of Ignoring These Legal Implications

If you choose to ignore the legal implications of mobile marketing or make a mistake without any ill intent, you are risking intervention from the FTC and/or your state attorney general. A violation could lead to a cease-and-desist order. You might also have to provide corrective advertising as part of your consequences. You also may face a fine, which could be significant. The CAN-SPAM Act penalties are as high as $11,000 per violation. Of course, you are also open to a lawsuit if you ignore the laws that are set forth to protect consumers from deceptive mobile marketers. Make sure that you are following every law that is set in motion. Not only is it smart marketing, it is smart business.

Tips for Getting Your Mobile Campaign through Your Legal Department

One of the most common issues faced by marketing departments is how to get their concepts through the legal department. This is especially true with mobile marketing since it is so new. Legal departments often don't know what to make of mobile marketing initiatives. My best advice is to get and follow the MMA's Best Practices document (see the sidebar on page 48) when you are building your campaign. Then submit that document along with the campaign so that your legal department can see that you have followed the guidelines. Just be sure to get the most updated version of the document. The best practices are now reviewed and updated by the MMA every six months. As the industry gains solid ground, the best practices will not change as often. Reviewing the document and ensuring that your campaign aligns with it should go a long way toward working well with your legal department.

Chapter Updates and Online Resource Guide

Updates to this chapter and its related Online Resource Guide are available at www.mobilemarketinghandbook.com/Updates/Legal.

The Online Resource Guide for Chapter 3 includes links for all sites listed in this chapter.

Resources

The following resources are included to help you with further research and/or implementation of the ideas found in this chapter.

Mobile Marketing Best Practices

MMA Consumer Best Practices Guidelines,
    www.mmaglobal.com/bestpractices.pdf

Free Privacy Policy Templates

Better Business Bureau Sample Privacy Notice,
    www.bbbonline.org/privacy/sample_privacy.asp
Perfectly Private: Private Policy Template,
    www.perfectlyprivate.com/easy_template.shtml

Privacy Policy Consultants

Alan Chapell, Chapell & Associates, LLC,
 www.chapell associates.com

U.S. Law Firms/Attorneys

Gary Kibel, Davis & Gilbert LLP, www.dglaw.com
Todd D. Daubert, Kelley Drye & Warren LLP, www.kelleydrye.com

Canadian Law Firms/Attorneys

Eric Swetsky, MBA, LLB, www.advertisinglawyer.ca

Launching Your Campaign

Launching a mobile campaign is rewarding because when it's mobile ... people talk.

—Jared Reitzin, CEO, mobileStorm, Inc.

You are ready to choose your mobile marketing tool(s) and launch your campaign when the following three conditions are met: 1) You determine that your customer base is mobile-savvy (as outlined in Chapter 1), 2) you figure out the value you will offer to your customers, and 3) you align that value with your company's desired outcome (from Chapter 2).

Three Paths to Your Mobile Launch

There are three paths to launching your mobile campaign and which you choose is likely to depend upon the size of your business and your budget. First, major corporations and brand managers will undoubtedly be working with an agency to implement their mobile campaigns since they already have agencies working on their other advertising efforts. Second, marketing managers of mid-sized companies, agency employees, media properties including magazines and newspapers, and even small companies with a significant budget will be working directly with mobile vendors to launch their campaigns. They may use the services of a mobile consultant to facilitate the strategy and launch but then continue on with the campaign on their own. Third, small businesses, Internet marketers, bloggers, and other entrepreneurs are likely to use the do-it-yourself guerrilla marketing approach. The do-it-yourselfers will probably need significant education and coaching, but it is possible. There is nothing right or wrong about which path is chosen, but each path has certain points that are important to note as you proceed with the launch of your campaign.

Working with an Agency

If you are already working with an agency, you should ask what it is currently doing for your company and about the firm's expertise in the mobile arena before assuming that it can handle your mobile campaign. If you are satisfied that it has real knowledge in mobile marketing and the capacity to handle your campaign, you will want to work with your current agency on your mobile as well. After all, your mobile campaign needs to be integrated with your other efforts, so it makes sense to have one entity coordinating all of it. If your current agency doesn't have enough experience with mobile or doesn't yet offer services in the mobile area, look for a specialized mobile marketing agency.

How to Know If Your Current Agency Can Handle Mobile

To determine if your current agency can handle a mobile campaign, ask what mobile campaigns the firm has already launched. You want to know that you are not the firm's first mobile campaign, and you'd like to find out how successful other mobile campaigns have been. Also find out what the firm's staffing capacity is for mobile. You want it to have staff dedicated to working in mobile. It is a unique tool and not just something that can easily be added on to an already full job description. Be sure to see the list of discussion points in the next section about choosing a mobile agency, vendor, or consultant. These points will help you choose a new agency or ensure your current one is a good match for mobile.

How to Choose a Mobile Agency, Vendor, or Consultant

When you contact a company for your mobile marketing campaign (whether it is a text message company, an agency, a multiplatform vendor, or a consultant), you want the company to be qualified to work on mobile campaigns. Here are some discussion points that any firm should initiate. You should be ready to discuss all these points, but pay attention to whether the company actually introduces these topics. Their not doing so shows you that you have not found the right company to help you with your mobile campaign.

- The company should ask about goals and then offer input on whether your requests are realistic. Many times, potential clients will ask for something unrealistic, and an honest, ethical vendor will let clients know they are over reaching, even if they run the risk of losing the business.

- A potential vendor should ask about your ideas for mobile. Since it is such a new industry, it is always good to get ideas from whoever has them. Creativity can also come from the client. Once the ideas have been shared, a vendor should help determine if the campaign complies with all the Mobile Marketing Association (MMA) Best Practices.

- The vendor should ask about your customer base and how mobile-savvy that base is. Maybe the vendor will suggest that customers conduct a survey of their clients to gauge their interest in interacting with the company on mobile.

- The agency or vendor should be willing to share information about similar campaigns the firm has handled. The quality of these campaigns should be evident by how well they worked technologically as well as from the actual results (if the vendor is able to share that information).

- Lastly, the vendor should inquire about the budget, how much is being allocated to promoting the mobile campaign, and what the promotional plans are for the project, including any promotional partners on board. Any vendor can sell the technology to make a campaign happen, but only ethical ones care how it turns out. Knowing that a client has a solid promotional campaign to support a mobile initiative is part of its overall success; the firm should be asking about it.

What You Need to Know About Working with an Agency

If you work with an agency, you will need to arrive on the doorstep armed with your goals and desired outcomes from mobile. You'll need to share what resources you can allocate to your mobile campaign, and then let the agency handle the strategy and implementation. Since mobile can revitalize other marketing efforts, it might be wise to discuss which of your current marketing may be underperforming. It is possible that you can turn them around by introducing mobile as a direct response tool to those marketing efforts.

Since mobile is a marketing tool that must be well integrated into your other marketing efforts (more on this in Chapter 5), an agency can take care of integrating it for you. If the agency is already managing your Internet, print campaign, or TV and radio spots, it can easily add in the mobile campaign to those ads.

Budget Guidelines for Working with an Agency

You will work directly with your agency on the specific budget for mobile, but you also need to budget for ancillary items such as promotion for your mobile campaign. Integrating it into your current marketing budget will only go so far; you will need to set aside funds specifically to alert your customers that your mobile campaign exists. Your agency will be able to suggest the proper amount based on the campaign you choose to launch. Chapter 5 covers promoting your mobile campaigns in detail.

It is also likely that you will have to initiate staff training to close the circle on mobile. For example, if your agency decides to offer a mobile coupon, you will need to ensure that your staff who will be accepting these mobile coupons are thoroughly trained. Additionally, your order processing equipment (cash registers, accounting software, and so on) will need to work with your mobile offering. You'll also need to account for these costs in your budget.

What You Need to Know About Working with a Vendor

To implement a mobile campaign, you will need to work with vendors including text message companies, ad networks, and mobile web builders. (See the sidebar on page 62 for more types of mobile marketing vendors.) However, an agency will manage these relationships for you, and it's likely that you won't have any direct contact with your mobile marketing vendors. If you are not working with an agency (or you *are* the agency), you will be working directly with these vendors who are experts and will guide you through the entire mobile maze. Even though it is not the same as working with an agency that handles every last detail, you can count on your vendors to uphold their part of the campaign and quite possibly enhance the strategic planning as well.

If you go directly to a vendor or group of vendors, you should have already formulated your overall mobile marketing strategy and know where you expect each particular vendor to fit into that strategy. It will be your responsibility to coordinate multiple vendors and to ensure that it is all working smoothly with your other marketing. Your chosen vendors will be able to help out somewhat with these tasks, but remember only you will have a vision of the big picture. They will ensure that their part of the campaign goes smoothly and that everything associated with it is handled.

Budget Guidelines for Working with Vendors

Because you are not paying someone else for the strategy and integration with your other marketing, your out-of-pocket investment is typically much less than working with an agency. Your only costs are for vendor services. The range of your budget will depend on the type of mobile services you are using. A stand-alone text message campaign is on the lower end of the price range, and the higher end offers a comprehensive mobile site, mobile advertising, and additional marketing efforts to support your mobile campaign. Similarly to how the Internet vendors transformed over time, expect to see prices for web-building services decrease and prices for mobile advertising increase. Text message rates are likely to be the most stable because that technology is the most widely used and may have already stabilized.

Frequently Asked Questions of Agencies and Vendors

While interviewing agencies and vendors for this book, I compiled a list of the most common questions clients and potential clients asked them. Even if you are doing it yourself, you'll still need to know the answers to these questions:

How can I get a list of cell phone numbers to start a mobile campaign?

You can't. As Chris Torbit from Blast Companies tells everyone who asks him this question, "Everybody starts at zero." There are no lists of mobile phone numbers you can buy, rent, or use to start marketing with mobile. You have to build your own list by getting your customers to opt in or ask you. But you do have your existing customer lists with email, phone, and mail addresses. You can start your mobile campaign by reaching out to this group and enticing them to opt in with the value via mobile. Your mobile list will begin to grow, and you will be on your way to launching a successful mobile marketing campaign.

Why should I consider mobile as part of my marketing mix?

The answer to this question is not simple. In some cases, mobile is not the right channel to use, but in others, it is the perfect choice. Mobile is a good option to add to your marketing mix if there is a combination of the following: a mobile-savvy audience; a compelling reason for them to interact with you, such as the good value you will provide; the right technology to carry out your idea; and a promotional plan to make the launch a success. With these key ingredients, you can create a solid mobile marketing strategic plan combining all of those ingredients. Consider mobile as part of your marketing mix because it brings added life and interaction into your existing campaigns. It can help you turn some of your one-way marketing channels into direct response tools. Mobile is the newest mass media, and you will not want to miss out on participating in the dawn of this powerful medium. (See the Appendix at the end of this book for a detailed description of the seven mass media, of which mobile is the seventh.)

What are the success measurements in mobile marketing?

I am glad to see that measuring success is one of the topics that people ask about. It means marketers are creating campaigns that produce results. However, there are so many ways to measure success objectively with mobile that I can't figure out why they even have to ask. From mobile (voice) to text messaging to the mobile web, almost every technology you would ask a customer to use is trackable. You can count exactly how many incoming calls came from a mobile campaign, how many text messages were sent, and how many mobile coupons were received and then redeemed. Even on the mobile web, you can develop a robust set of data that will tell you everything you need to know about your campaign's success. Your agency and your mobile vendors will be able to provide objective details you can use. But what you may not know is what success is typical. The new technology does not have clear-cut benchmarks established or widely known. You just have to jump in, test the waters, and measure success by your standards. See Chapter 6 for more details on tracking and analyzing your mobile campaign.

In addition to the mobile vendor fees, you need to include a promotion budget to announce your mobile marketing campaign to the world. Chapter 5 covers the process of marketing your mobile campaign, and the bottom line is that you can't do much of anything without promotion allocated into the budget. You probably already have budgets for other marketing campaigns, and you can certainly integrate the mobile call-to-action into those other media without adding substantially to the budget. You just have to account for it and plan on it.

Do-It-Yourself Using Guerrilla Tactics

Small businesses with limited budgets, bloggers, Internet marketers, and other entrepreneurs who are used to getting their hands dirty implementing every step of their own campaigns will be happy to know that they can tackle mobile using guerrilla tactics. You should also know that it is not particularly easy; mobile is trickier because it is so new with so many variables (hundreds of handsets, and dozens of browsers and operating systems, not to mention working with the carriers). The tools are not as self-explanatory as many Internet tools are; you have to know mobile marketing well to use them. It is possible to forge ahead on your own; just be sure you study mobile marketing strategies thoroughly (including those found in this book). Realistically speaking, a world of frustration and wasted time and money awaits you if you don't.

What You Need to Know about Doing It Yourself Using Guerrilla Tactics

Businesses of any size with the ability to conduct smaller campaigns using fewer resources (i.e., guerrilla marketing) will be able to launch in mobile faster and with less red tape than companies that use agencies. The agency route will undoubtedly take your agency-ready colleagues down the path of leasing their own short code (see Chapter 8 for info on what that means), doing a multimedia launch, and building an enterprise-worthy mobile site, and they will likely invest quite a bit of money and time in mobile just to get started. But on your own you can start with a simple text message campaign (working with a shared short code vendor) and integrate the campaign into the marketing you are already doing. Your upfront costs will be low, and you can get started quickly. It is likely that your mobile marketing campaign will already be launched by the time larger companies working with agencies have finished their first round of committee meetings to decide about their mobile strategy. But this is not unique to mobile; this is simply one of the huge advantages small businesses have over large corporations.

Types of Mobile Marketing Vendors

You may be wondering exactly what types of vendors you'll be working with in your mobile campaign development. You may not be working with every one of these types, but the following list features the categories of vendors you will encounter and what they do in mobile:

- Short code providers – Lease short codes (the five- to six-digit number used in text message campaigns that are leased by the companies who market with the code).

- Aggregators – Provide the technological and relationship link between cell phone carriers and text message companies.

- Text message companies – Offer the software back end that allows agencies and companies to run text message campaigns, which can be managed services or self-service.

- Mobile website designers – Work specifically with mobile web.

- Mobile website builders – Not vendors per se, but a service you can use to build a mobile website. These can be free, low cost, or offered by vendors who license the use of their site building system to you.

- Ad networks – Match advertisers with publishers, giving advertisers a place to serve their ads (on their publishers' sites) and giving publishers a way to monetize their mobile websites.

- Mobile marketing consultants – Aid businesses in strategizing and launching mobile campaigns by matching companies with the right vendors to implement mobile campaigns.

To use the do-it-yourself method of mobile marketing, you or someone on your team needs to be tech-savvy. You'll need to know how to sign up for a variety of recommended web-based programs such as text message software and website builders, run online ad campaigns, put web analytics code onto your site, and integrate everything into your other marketing. A solid foundation of Internet marketing know-how will serve you well. However, you will also need to give up some of the beliefs you have about how things work. Mobile marketing, although similar in many ways, is different from Internet marketing.

Tips for Doing It Yourself

The price to be paid for doing it yourself is a big investment in implementation time and the learning curve. That is not to say it's impossible, but for any savings you want to realize on vendor services, you must make up for with your own blood, sweat, and tears. By adhering to the following pointers, you will dramatically reduce that pain:

- Use mobile-specific tools. Some of the ones you use (and take for granted) on the Internet, including Google Analytics, do not work on mobile. Also, mobile website building is, ironically, fairly complicated and requires following exact protocols. See Chapter 9 for more details.

- The do-it-yourself tools do not have all the kinks and technical glitches worked out. This is especially true of mobile website builders, each of which has a variety of features, some of which work more soundly than others. In all fairness, even if the site builders work perfectly, there are still likely to be some technical glitches that will happen on the carrier level or because of browser or handset difficulties. For example, your carefully crafted mobile site might show up perfectly and beautifully on the Sprint network, but Verizon subscribers won't see it at all.

- Text message platforms are stable but still have a range of capabilities from vendor to vendor. You need to know what features and functionality you will need before you decide which vendor to choose. See Chapter 8 for details.

- Don't be tempted to build your own platforms! It is more complicated than you think. For example, it is not that technically difficult to build an email-based text message system (using SMTP technology), but it is unwise. Not only is this technology notoriously unreliable, but it is not in line with mobile marketing best practices. This means your entire campaign can be brought down in a flick of a switch *without notice* from any one or all of the mobile carriers. The only way to have a commercially viable text message program is through short codes. See Chapter 8 for details.

- With the exception of Internet service providers (ISPs) being able to block emails from you, you are not used to outside influences having control of your campaigns as an Internet marketer. In mobile, the carriers have quite a bit of control from having total approval of leased short code campaigns to being able to shut down any campaign that goes across their networks. Additionally, the Federal Trade Commission is carefully monitoring mobile marketing and expects strict adherence to the MMA Best Practices, as described in Chapter 3. These best practices apply to you as uniformly as they do large corporations, and you are well advised to follow them or risk ruining your entire mobile approach.

Budget Guidelines for Using Do-It-Yourself Guerrilla Marketing Tactics

As with anything you do yourself, there are costs involved: your time, the opportunity cost of investing your time in learning something new, and even the unavoidable out-of-pocket costs. There are a few low- or no-cost mobile marketing tools that you can use to launch your mobile campaign (see the Resources list at the end of this chapter). You can spend next to nothing on a free ad-based text message service such as TextMarks and build your mobile site with free mobile site builders, for example. A word of caution: You get what you pay for. Sometimes free is not the best option. As we go through the book, I'll share low- and no-cost resources with you for each tool, and let you know if they are professional enough to stake your reputation on for your marketing.

By following the strategies and guidelines in this book and using the resources in the Online Resource Guide, you can use a mobile website builder to create a basic mobilized website and submit your site to the mobile search engines yourself. Likewise, you can start a mobile advertising campaign using the self-service options available from the mobile ad net-works found in this book in Chapter 10. Once your site is active, you can sign up for the free mobile analytical software and start tracking your campaigns and your return on investment (ROI).

The process of launching your mobile campaign will be more challenging from day to day than I just outlined, but there are affordable tools and vendors that can open mobile marketing to just about anyone with any budget. You can always get help and further your education (see my blog for options at www.mobilemarketingprofits.com), consulting and getting help from a mobile marketing launch specialist.

Launching your mobile campaign is exciting and tedious at the same time. There are details to handle, relationships to manage, strategies to plan, and finally a campaign to execute. All of this must be done with the clear knowledge of mobile marketing's quirks and requirements. There are just so many nuances, legalities, and confounding issues to deal with, and there is no need for you to tackle it alone. Here's where to get help. Individual vendors are listed at the end of each chapter in Part 2.

Chapter Updates and Online Resource Guide

Updates to this chapter and its related Online Resource Guide are available at www.mobilemarketinghandbook.com/Updates/Launching.

The Online Resource Guide for Chapter 4 includes links for all sites listed in this chapter.

Resources

The following resources are included to help you with further research and/or implementation of the ideas found in this chapter.

Mobile Marketing Agencies

3Cinteractive, www.3cinteractive.com
HipCricket, www.hipcricket.com
ipsh!, www.ipsh.net
mobileStorm, www.mobilestorm.com
Punchkick Interactive, www.punchkickinteractive.com

Mobile Marketing Consultants

Tomi T Ahonen, www.tomiahonen.com
Karla Allen, Direct Mobile Partners, directmobilepartners.com
Alan Moore, SMLXL, www.smlxtralarge.com

Marketing Your Mobile Campaign

The interactivity of the mobile phone will make legacy media come alive. TV, radio, print and billboards can all be made interactive with mobile, bringing out new forms of advertising even in old media. Mobile will be woven into the center of most campaigns and no longer isolated to tiny mobile-specific islands.
— Chetan Sharma, *Mobile Advertising*

80/20 Rule and Creating Synergy

With mobile marketing, customers must take action to accept marketing, and that action on their part is sparked by marketing on your part. After you have built your mobile presence or created a mobile marketing campaign, you will have to raise awareness about your campaign if it is to succeed. You can make your customers aware of your campaign by integrating it into your other marketing to achieve your desired outcome. As a powerful mass media, mobile does not work well in a vacuum. It is imperative to use other marketing tools to drive consumer participation in mobile campaigns. It is only through effective marketing integration that mobile is effective as a marketing tool. As an example, businesses cannot just start sending out messages to a list of cell phones; a text message campaign takes some outreach, such as a sign, advertisement, or other announcement to get customers to participate. A mobile website requires traffic-generating work, including search engine optimization (SEO), mobile advertising, publicity, or putting your mobile site on your printed marketing materials to get visitors. It obviously requires other marketing efforts to help your customers discover your mobile campaigns.

In case you think that marketing your mobile campaign is a mere afterthought, think about this version of the 80/20 principle. Lining up the technology behind your mobile marketing campaign is 20 percent of your work; the remaining 80 percent is all about the planning and marketing of the campaign. It is ironic that the success of a mobile marketing campaign depends on its marketing; however, it is easier to understand the concept when you consider that adding a mobile component to other marketing actually improves that marketing. For example, a billboard embedded with a mobile coupon generates immediate trackable sales instead of just drive-by brand awareness. It is synergy at its best. The combined effort of mobile added to your original marketing effort is stronger than it would be alone. You may find that your marketing becomes so entangled that you don't know if you are marketing your mobile campaign or using mobile as a direct response tool to enhance your other marketing. Either way is fine.

In many ways, mobile is the key that unlocks each of the other media's true potential. A marketing campaign that customers can immediately interact with and that is in a multitude of environments is one that can be truly successful. That is what mobile brings to the table and in a big way. Incorporating a mobile response mechanism in your other marketing can help make all your other efforts more effective because they become imme-diately actionable by your customers. One example of this is a bus stop bench ad for a real estate agent. Without a mobile component, these bench ads are brand-awareness tools. The agent is hoping that people who see the name in the ad will recognize the name in the future when they need to buy or sell a house. If the ad included a text message campaign such as "Text LISTINGS to 12345 to find out what houses are for sale in the area," the bus bench ad has now become an interactive resource for the home buyers. It has also become a better-bang-for-the-buck marketing tool for the real estate agent. By analyzing the response rates of a series of ads, you can determine which ones bring in the most and best leads. This tracking of the responses now makes the bus ads a valuable business analysis tool as well.

Integrating Mobile into All Other Marketing

When you launch a mobile marketing campaign, launch it with gusto. Inform your customers about it in all of your current marketing methods. Make sure your salespeople know about it and tell their customers. Add it to all your other marketing: ads, radio spots, email campaigns, in-store sign-age, billboards, flyers, company newsletter, publicity campaigns, and web-site. It should be impossible for anyone who sees your marketing or interacts with your business in any way to miss the launch of your mobile marketing campaign. If you have created your mobile campaign correctly, it will provide value to your customers; they will want to know about it. Following are some ways you can market your mobile campaign.

Papa John's Excellent Adventure in Mobile Marketing

Throughout this chapter, I'll be using a Papa John's Pizza mobile marketing campaign as a working example. The campaign being referenced is the launch of Papa John's campaign to order pizza via text message. This campaign, which was announced in November 2007, is a well-integrated mobile marketing campaign and makes a high-quality example. Because I am a Papa John's customer, I personally received some of the marketing messages. But that is not the sole reason I am aware of this campaign; I also saw the extensive media coverage and blogs about it. Papa John's Pizza called upon Fleishman-Hillard, its branding and public relations agency, to devise a strategy that gives us an excellent example of how to market a mobile marketing initiative.

Word of Mouth

Positive word of mouth (people telling their friends about a product/service they liked and then giving a recommendation for it) is one of the most powerful persuasion techniques known. According to the Word of Mouth Marketing Association, the marketing practice is "Giving people a reason to talk about your products and services, and making it easier for that conversation to take place." By definition, word-of-mouth marketing is not something that can be controlled or manipulated, but you certainly can and should take proactive steps to help your mobile campaign get recognition. Here are some good word-of-mouth marketing approaches you can take when promoting your campaign.

Sparking Word of Mouth

The trick to word-of-mouth marketing is that you can't make it happen. You can only make it easy for it to happen. Start by creating a mobile campaign worth sharing and talking about. If you don't do this, nothing else you try in relation to word-of-mouth marketing will work. Then build ways into your campaign for your customers to share it. The tell-a-friend concept is powerful, and sometimes all it takes is giving people a way to do so and it happens. Wherever you can throughout your campaign make it easy for people to share what they are experiencing with your company via mobile. A smart example of this is Redbox's Free Movie Monday offer. Customers can sign up to get a text message every Monday for a free movie from Redbox. Here's what those messages look like:

> Redbox free MONDAY rental. CHECK OUT WITH COUPON DM1048. Expires at midnight 05-12-08. Fwd to friends. Call 866-733-2693 for help. Text STOP to quit.

I would have never thought about forwarding my coupon code to friends, but the fact that Redbox mentioned it actually alerted me to the opportunity that I could share this free movie offer. So I did. Actually, I have also told numerous people about it verbally, and I've posted it on Twitter several times, blogged about it, and have now featured it in this book. This campaign is done well and worth sharing.

Word of Mouth Starts at Home

Since your customers interact with your call center and salespeople regularly, these staff members are often the primary point of contact with your company. Make sure they are fully aware of everything you are doing, especially mobile marketing campaigns. A new mobile marketing campaign is the perfect topic for them to share with your customers. Give them talking points they can use to discuss your mobile campaign when speaking with customers. It could be as simple as suggesting they say, "Did you know that you can get [share the benefit to the customer here] from us by [describe how to participate]?" Have your staff ask customers whether they have visited the company's mobile website yet and then share something with them that will make it worth their time to do so. Often giving people specific ideas of when and where they will find it useful to use your mobile site will be just what they need to hear. Leveraging your employees' interaction with your customers is likely to be one of your most effective methods to drive people into your mobile campaign.

Online Marketing

There are many ways to market your mobile campaign online, including promoting your mobile campaign on your company website, leveraging the power of bloggers to get the word out, and launching an online advertising campaign about it.

Integration with Your Company Website

How many visitors come to your website? Every one of them should see an opportunity to participate in your mobile marketing campaign. This is a no-brainer when it comes to integration strategy. Not only can website exposure lead people into your mobile campaign, but it can also help them participate when they see it somewhere else. People are used to a website being a repository for all things related to a particular company. If they need to know more about what you are doing with mobile, they will go to your website. This is the perfect spot to post ways to participate in your mobile campaign.

Offer your website visitors the choice of opting into your text message campaign from your website. They don't have to do it just from their cell phones. This keeps them interacting with you where they are most comfortable. It also leads visitors from interacting with you in one form of communication channel into another. You can do this by getting the widget code from your text message vendor, or your agency can do it for you. Be sure to include specific instructions about how to participate with your mobile campaign. Remember: Your audience may need help and guidance, especially if you are trying to reach beyond the under-30 market.

Having a send-to-mobile option on your website is one way to connect people to you in their mobile world. This technology will send a text message to their phones with either what they want or a link to it. The option is convenient for the customers, makes the search easy for them, and eliminates the chance they will forget about your campaign once they log off your website. After all, the message will be waiting for them on their phones. Customers are already starting to see this on sites such as MapQuest, Weather.com, and YellowPages.com. Consumers will soon begin to look for it everywhere.

Start by putting a mobile option on your maps/directions page, contact page, or anything that people are likely to want sent to their mobile from your site. Since this is going to involve sending texts to multiple carriers, you will need to have your own short code. Or you can use a service especially designed for this, such as zipwhip.com, that has a quick and easy way to add the short code to your site if you don't have your own. Note that this is not something you can build for yourself and make it work. It is not an Internet technology; it is a mobile one.

Leveraging the Power of Bloggers

Blog readers and bloggers are typically tech-savvy folks, and because of that, they are also likely to participate in mobile campaigns. In addition to getting consumers to participate in your campaign, blogging can help you garner offline media exposure. The Papa John's campaign included a blogger outreach component that helped the company get coverage in two national magazines. Blogs featured the news about its new text-to-order pizza capability. Writers from national magazines read the story in the blogs and then covered the story in their publications.

So if you already have a company blog, be sure to post entries about your new campaign. If you are not blogging yet (yes, even if you are from a big corporation), you need to start. It is an extremely powerful marketing tool online.

In addition to announcing your campaign on your own blog, share the news of your campaign with other bloggers who cover your topic or who share the same audience. You can do this by contacting bloggers with whom you have already established a relationship through commenting on their blogs, linking to their blog in posts on your blog, or in some other way. A blog announcement campaign can do wonders for your marketing, but you must approach bloggers in a way that works for them. A mass email to a list of bloggers won't work. They need to be contacted individually and personally for your outreach to have any effect.

Advertising Online

Advertising on blogs for your mobile campaign is also a good way to get the word out. You can either contact bloggers directly about placing an ad on their sites, or you can work through a blog ad network. If a blog is a good match for your audience (for example, if your campaign will appeal to busy moms, then use a mom-oriented blog) and the blog already has ads on it, look for an "Advertise Here" link or page. If you want to go through an ad network, you can use the network's services to place ads for you on the blogs that they represent. You'll work directly with them, and they will coordinate with the blogs handling ad placement and payment. Some reputable blog ad networks include FeedBurner, Federated Media Publishing, Blogads, and b5media.

You can also launch a pay-per-click ad campaign (Google AdWords, Yahoo! Search Engine Marketing, or MSN's Microsoft adCenter) to promote your mobile offering. This Internet pay-per-click campaign would drive traffic to your desktop website. From your full-size site, you can encourage participation in your mobile campaign. Make sure if you do this you create a special landing page (a web page specifically designed to be the first page visitors see when they click on an ad) that is focused on your mobile campaign. If you promote the mobile campaign in a pay-per-click ad, the visitor should be directed to it from the first click without having to search around your site for it.

Email

Another absolute must is to announce your mobile campaign to your email list. If you have an email list for your regular communications, send out a few email alerts to announce your mobile marketing campaign. Papa John's did it. A few hours after Papa John's posted the media release, I received an email announcing the new way to order pizza. Here was the subject line:

Order your Pizza with a Text Message! New from Papa John's.

It makes sense to tell people who already communicate with you about a new way to work with your company. You should keep reminding people in subsequent emails, too. Not every email is opened, so you shouldn't assume that announcing it one time has saturated your email readers. In fact, you will likely see your response increase the more often you include information about your mobile campaign in your email newsletters, announcements, and other communications. Don't overdo it, either; just include the news of your mobile offering in multiple emails according to your usual email publication schedule.

Signage

Signage (billboards, posters, banners, or signs inside your place of business) can drive a tremendous mobile response. The beauty of using signs to market your mobile campaign is that the people you want to engage with your mobile marketing efforts are actually mobile when they see these signs. The flip side is that mobile brings signs to life; signs embedded with a mobile call-to-action become direct response marketing.

Signage/Mobile Integration Tips

To make the best use of integrating your signs and mobile campaign, consider the following tips:

- Put your call-to-action prominently on the sign. It should be obvious that you want the sign reader to do something as a result of seeing the sign besides just reading it and passing by.

- Give people a reason to participate. Spell out the value they will receive by participating. They should tell at a glance what benefits they will receive by participating. It should be easy for them to figure out what you are asking them to do.

- Include a mobile phone graphic to help people realize that you are suggesting they use their phones to respond. Until mobile is completely ingrained in people's minds, you may need to help them think it through. Once the Mobile Marketing Association's (MMA) industry use logo (see the end of this chapter for details) is available, you can use that. For now, include your own graphic.

How to Use Signs to Drive Mobile Response

Getting people to respond via mobile to your signs takes a bit of finesse and strong marketing. Here are some ideas for eliciting a response:

- Let people register or RSVP for an upcoming event. This could be done via a text message, by posting a mobile website that people could use to send in their name and reservation, by using a 2D bar code for them to scan to get a VIP code immediately, or by offering a phone number they can call immediately to register.

- Share your mobile coupon offers and experience an immediate response to your signs. By offering different coupons, you can track which signs are bringing you the most business. You can also increase the participation in your mobile coupon campaign by marketing it with signs.

- Entice passers-by to turn on their Bluetooth to receive a multimedia message from your business. (See Chapter 12 for details.)

Advertising

Unless you are a major brand or have a major budget, you probably won't launch an ad campaign just to tout your mobile campaign. But you certainly should add mobile as a direct response to your existing ad campaigns, whatever their reach.

Magazine/Newspaper Advertising

While it may seem odd at first to incorporate mobile response into print ads, keep in mind that people keep their mobile phones close by them even when they are at home. A person curled up on the couch reading the newspaper is more likely to have a mobile device instead of a computer near them, so don't hesitate to put your mobile call-to-action in your print ads. You never know where someone might be when he or she is reading the paper. This is an ideal time to add your 2D bar code (more on these in Chapter 12) so your audience can quickly and easily get to your mobile site with a quick snap of a photo or by inserting your short code to sign them up for your text club, a series of text messages that are sent out on a regular basis. If you have a mobile campaign, there aren't many scenarios where you shouldn't include your mobile call-to-action, the specific action a marketer wants a consumer to take as a result of their marketing efforts.

Radio

Businesses including a call-to-action in radio ads have been big money makers for decades. In the good ol' days of home radio, people were encouraged to mail in their requests, much as Ralphie did in the classic movie *A Christmas Story*. Ralphie listened to the "Little Orphan Annie" show every day. Then he ordered a secret decoder kit so he could decipher a secret message that was shared on the air. He requested and received his decoder kit through the mail, but the magic was the interaction of having the kit in front of him while he listened to the show. But much to Ralphie's dismay, the secret message was actually an ad to "Drink More Ovaltine." (The hidden message here is that your value can't be corrupted by your marketing, or it won't work.) When most people started listening to their car radios during their commute, vendors started giving out phone numbers on the air to get people to buy their wares. It was once a sure bet to make mega book sales by having an author interviewed on the radio and providing a toll-free 800 number to order the book.

Mobile marketing has emerged as another opportunity to match a call-to-action with radio. Just as the other methods of driving contact from the radio peaked and then dropped off, this will as well. So, if you want to try it, do it now. And don't disappoint your audience with the "Drink More Ovaltine" trick. It didn't work in the movie, and it won't work for you either. The following examples are some ideas for integrating radio and mobile:

- Radio listeners can be encouraged to "Text KEYWORD to 12345 to get (something they want) from (whoever is talking on air)," or they can be encouraged to call a number and receive a text message offer in return. Higher response rates, as much as a 10:1

ratio, have been realized when people call first and then receive a text.

- Advertisers can conclude ads with a mobile call-to-action. By putting different tracking methods in place (such as using different keywords), an advertiser can determine which radio station is getting the best response. You can also determine the best time of day to drive the most participation because the response is immediate.

Chapter 8 has more ideas for integrating text messaging with radio campaigns.

Television

Integrating mobile and TV can be more than just announcing your mobile campaign; in fact, mobile response to TV has one of the highest known mobile response rates. It all started in the U.S. with *American Idol*. According to Chetan Sharma in his book *Mobile Advertising,* the 2005 *American Idol* voting was the "single biggest TXT (test messaging) event in the world." Amazingly, the 41.5 million votes received via text came at a time when text messaging was largely unused in the U.S. market. By the 2006 season, 120 million votes were received by text message.

Of course, not every company blending TV and mobile will get these fantastic results, but there are plenty of ways for businesses to leverage the power of TV with mobile. It is clear that given the right incentive people will participate. Just as commercials first started mentioning website addresses to drive Internet traffic, it is unusual and exciting to see a mobile call-to-action now. Take advantage of that while the novelty helps boost your response. Take a look at some of the following ideas for using TV and mobile together:

- Nonprofit and charitable organizations can have a text-to-donate option at the end of their ads. This could considerably raise donations because it is completely quick and easy and wouldn't interrupt the viewers' TV watching.

- Musicians can fulfill immediate music downloads straight to mobile instead of suggesting a CD purchase at a store or an iTunes visit that will later have to be synced with a music player.

- Restaurants (fast food or the sit-down variety) can offer a mobile coupon. People who requested a mobile coupon and have it ready and waiting on their mobile devices are more likely to go to the restaurant they saw advertised than a passive viewer who had no interaction with the ad.

- Car dealerships can include an option to request a brochure or test drive immediately after seeing an ad for a car. A mobile site with a full features list and photos might also appeal to car shoppers.

- Pharmaceutical companies can offer to send a reminder text to "check with your doctor" about XYZ prescription.

- An interactive poll that gives viewers the opportunity to tell you what they think about a particular product or even the ad itself would be new and exciting. An ad filmed like a mini show can give viewers the chance to vote on the end of the story in an upcoming episode.

The options are endless and depend upon the creativity of your mobile strategy team to devise the right idea for your company. If you are already doing TV advertising, it is almost a no-brainer to integrate mobile. The companies that choose to jump in early with well-thought-out campaigns will win big time.

Trade Shows/Consumer Events

An industry trade show or consumer event (such as a bridal expo or holiday festival) can be the perfect place to market your mobile campaign; in fact, it might even be a good reason to launch one. Because your customers are physically gathered together for a specific purpose for a finite period of time, it is the ideal scenario to promote and run your mobile campaign. You can market your mobile campaign in a variety of ways, from pre-show advertising to on-the-floor promotions:

- In your trade show directory ad or pre-show trade magazine ads, ask people to sign up for a text message club so they can be updated on news or special events during the show.

- Create a series of value-packed text messages that can be sent at key times during the show. Be sure not to be too commercial or send only texts about your own company. Send information that trade show attendees will want to know about, including your own promotions.

- Help attendees more fully participate in the event by offering event details on your mobile website. You can distribute business cards with the mobile website address at your booth. Be sure to put some in the pressroom too.

- At a consumer event, you can encourage sign ups for your mobile coupon campaign, giving a free gift or on-the-spot discount to anyone who signs up.

- Signage around the event can direct attendees to your mobile campaign and will help increase booth traffic.

Be sure to see Chapter 11 for more ideas on using mobile marketing at trade shows.

Social Networking

Be sure to announce your mobile marketing campaign to your social networking circles including your Facebook friends and Twitter groups. First, if you are social networking correctly (see Chapter 11 for details), you will have a sizable following of those who communicate with you on a regular basis. Sharing the news about your campaign will simply be part of the conversation. Plus, the entire concept of social networking is for you to tell two friends, then for them to tell two friends, and so on. You never know who else might see it and jump on board. Social networking is an excellent way to market mobile campaigns.

Online Video

Marketing with YouTube and other online video sites is an art in itself, but it is a powerful one. It works well to create videos that tie into your mobile marketing campaign and promote them. As a part of their text message campaign launch, Papa John's created a text messaging versus ordering by phone showdown at the Mall of America on November 19, 2007. Fran Capo, the world's fastest talker, competed against Morgan Pozgar, the LG National Texting Champion, to see who could order a pizza faster. Capo called her order in; Pozgar sent in her order via text message. They posted the video of this at YouTube (youtube.com/watch?v=sFz81frZUBE); in the video, you can see that people were signing up on the spot for the online registration for text message ordering.

If you have a new mobile marketing campaign and want to show your customers how it works, you can create a video and post it on YouTube. Send the link to your customers via email. Ask your audience to go to

YouTube and search "name of video" to find help for getting through the procedure. You'll also probably get more folks finding you this way.

Product Packaging

Ever since kids started cutting the tops off of cereal boxes and mailing them in to cereal corporate headquarters to earn valuable prizes, there hasn't been a better way for consumers to interact with product packaging than with mobile. Not only can product packaging be a good way to promote mobile coupons and contests, it can also be an effective way to get consumer feedback. Any product that is highly portable, such as cups, is a good match for a mobile marketing campaign. After all, your customers are likely to have both necessary items (your product and their mobile devices) with them when you want them to take action. If you combine that with solid value, chances are you will stop seeing product packaging as a cost of goods expense and see it as marketing. (OK, for any accountants out there, I don't really mean that this be done in actual accounting. I'm just making a point.)

In some cases, incorporating mobile marketing into your product packaging can even help sell your product. If you have a product that generates pre-purchase questions or research, you can add a 2D bar code or mobile web link on the product package and explain that there are product reviews and an FAQ available. You could even offer a text message coupon on the package. By doing this, you help your customers gather all the information they need about your product, and you may entice them to buy your product using an interactive coupon.

Getting Publicity for Your Mobile Campaign

Before websites became common, it was not unusual for companies to get media coverage simply because they had a website. It seems laughable now, and no one would cover or mention an "ABC Company Develops Cool Website" story. However, while mobile marketing is still new, it will be possible to get coverage about your mobile marketing campaign just because you have one. A good example of this was Papa John's text message ordering capabilities for pizza. The company announced this new service on November 15, 2007. Within a few days, the *Wall Street Journal* and the Associated Press picked up the news. The story has been covered more than 817 times, including by newspapers across the country, on radio and TV hundreds of times, and on hundreds of blogs and websites. Even *People* and *Maxim* magazines covered the news.

At first, this kind of coverage will be possible to get on a nationwide basis, and then, as mobile marketing becomes more common, it will work only on a local level, and then it will begin to work only in niche or trade media. This will continue to work to get media coverage when the media is an exact match with your target market. For instance, a magazine that covers scrapbooking is likely to always cover a mobile campaign about scrapbooking. You will be able to get media coverage in marketing-oriented publications, but that won't help you unless your target audience is marketers.

Once the initial newsworthiness of mobile marketing campaigns wears off, the selling point will be what value is provided to the end consumer. And the first company to provide value in a significant way will reap the rewards of media exposure. The companies that come late to the table or provide no significant value will get nothing from the media. Mobile marketing strategies will simply no longer be newsworthy. If you are going to get media coverage for your mobile marketing campaign, you must take action and seek publicity now. If you don't have a publicist to handle this for you, here's a simple three-step guide to launching a publicity campaign to announce your mobile marketing campaign

Step 1: Build a Media List

You can announce your mobile marketing campaign by buying a media list or by creating one. If you buy one, make sure it is from a reputable source that provides frequent updates. Anything that provides less than monthly updates is outdated. If you create your own media list, start by compiling names and contact info for media that cover your topic. Working on a local campaign will be the easiest since you already know who covers your type of business. Find someone at each local TV channel, include the reporters at your city magazines, grab journalists' names from your daily newspaper, and be sure to get contacts at local weekly papers. You should also try to find any bloggers who cover your local market (just do a Google search for "your city name + blog"). With a little diligence, you will build a high-quality list fairly easily. It may not be a large list, but quality is more important anyway.

Step 2: Write a Media Release

A media release is a one-page document that reaches out to the media contacts on your list and to your customers through media release distribution points. Reporters, journalists, and producers use this release to decide whether to cover your story, and in some cases, they will use some of your wording to do so. Your customers will see your release as it is on the Internet, and it will help them decide to visit your website, call your business, or interact with your company through your mobile marketing campaign. To grab the reader's attention, create a media-worthy headline for your media release. "Media worthy" means that you write about what someone else wants to read and not what you are offering for sale. If you have built your mobile marketing campaign around the concept of providing value to the customer, you can use that strategy as your media-worthy angle as well. You will get media attention with headlines such as "XYZ Company Now Provides (Insert Customer Value Provided Here) through Mobile." Notice that it does not say "XYZ Company Launches New Mobile Marketing Campaign." There actually will be little interest that you launched a mobile marketing campaign, especially those on the receiving end of your marketing campaign.

Step 3: Distribute Your Media Release

Your media release can be mailed, emailed, or faxed to your handcrafted media list and submitted to wire services such as Business Wire, PR Newswire, and PRWeb. Ideally, try all of these options to maximize your exposure. PRWeb will also give you exposure to online search engines that can add your release to news searches. You will also want to post your media release in your online media room to give your website updated, add fresh content for the search engines to index, and provide exposure when media does a search for your topic.

College Marketing

It is no secret that younger mobile users are likely to be the most enthusiastic in mobile marketing. As long as part of your target market is college students, consider actively promoting your mobile marketing campaign to them using guerrilla marketing tactics on your local college campus or hiring a college marketing firm to create a nationwide campus campaign. Obviously, this will depend upon whether you have a local business or a nationwide company.

If you have a local business with personal access to a college campus, you can use grassroots campaign tactics quite easily and inexpensively. You can post flyers on campus billboards, speak at sororities and fraternities, sponsor a function or speech, send a media release to the school newspaper, or even give away T-shirts with your mobile marketing message (when students wear the T-shirts to class, your business is being marketed). You can also create a social networking persona to interact with students. (See more about social networking with mobile in Chapter 11.) You can also advertise in the college newspaper and send media releases to the college newspaper about newsworthy events, including the launch of your mobile campaign.

Mobile Marketing for Your Mobile Marketing

One way to market your mobile technology campaign is through mobile "moving" marketing. Anywhere people in your target market are gathering or walking around, you can market to them with movable signs. On behalf of MGM Grand, mobileStorm designed such a campaign. A billboard was transported down the Las Vegas strip where thousands of people were walking up and down the street. The sign invited people to send a text message with a short code to place their names on a VIP list for a party at a night club.

A local restaurant can accomplish a similar tactic at a local arts and crafts fair or local festival by hiring or recruiting 10 to 20 people (or more for a big event) to walk around the fair in matching T-shirts with a text message coupon offer on the back of the shirts. The repetition of the matching T-shirts would catch people's attention, and the uniqueness of the offer would create the response. The point is to reach people and interact with them while they are moving around with their mobile devices. If you provide value to the customer and make them aware of it, you have a winning recipe. When Amazon.com first started, the company representatives attended BookExpo America, the book industry's biggest U.S. trade show, and had dozens of people roaming the trade show floor in bright purple T-shirts. Amazon was quite visible at that show. Think about how much more powerful that marketing could have been if Amazon included a mobile offer on the back of each shirt. Such a large company can even have several offers going at the same time; people would naturally try to "collect" the offers.

Educating Your Customers on Using Mobile

For now, you may need to educate your customers on how to participate with mobile so your campaigns work. If your customers don't already know how to send a text message, spell it out for them step by step. If the mobile web is completely foreign to them, give them a little primer. Social networking is likely to take a bit of education on your part if you want to benefit from it. But it will be worth it. If you are the first one to introduce them to the technology and how to use it, your customers will be interacting with your company first.

Figure 5.1   This is an example of what text could be displayed on T-shirts for use as part of your mobile marketing strategy.

Explaining How to Send a Text Message

Author's Note: You have permission to use this wording in your marketing materials.

To send a text message, go to the Messaging center on your phone (it might be called something different on your phone). Find the option to Send a Message or Send a Text, and then start that process. In the space where you input who/what number to send the message, this is where you type in the short code (list your short code here in the text). The body of the message is where you put in the keyword (insert your keyword here). Then hit the Send button.

Standard messaging rates apply. This means we will not charge you any fee to send this message or to get the reply from us. If you have a text message plan, these texts will count as part of the number of your allocated text messages. If you don't have a text message plan, your cell phone company will charge you for each text message that is sent. This usually costs about 15 to 20 cents per text message.

Mobile Industry Logo Use

The MMA is designing a logo for all businesses involved in mobile marketing. The logo, actually a series of them, will be used in marketing campaigns to alert consumers that a mobile campaign is available. For a sign with a text message call-to-action, you would use the logo for text message campaigns and then choose a version of it based on whether it was a standard rate or premium campaign. For example, if you were driving traffic to a mobile website, you would use the logo for mobile web. Consumers will begin to recognize each of the logos as a way to interact more easily with mobile marketing. They will know whether they need to open their mobile browsers or send a text message. They can also tell if a campaign will be free or fee-based. You can think of it as similar to the movie rating system (G, PG, PG-13, and R) with a standardized logo that is instantly recognizable.

Using the mobile industry logo will help consumers understand your campaigns better; it is also likely that the logo will become a mandatory industry standard because the MMA will adopt it as a Best Practice. This means carriers will crack down on non-complying companies, and short codes can be shut down. Although it may take a while for it to become as widely known as the movie-rating system, the more businesses that use it, the quicker it will be adopted. At this early stage, the easier we can make it for consumers, the better it will be for everyone.

Chapter Updates and Online Resource Guide

Updates to this chapter and its related Online Resource Guide are available at www.mobilemarketinghandbook.com/Updates/Marketing.

The Online Resource Guide for Chapter 5 includes links for all sites listed in this chapter, as well as:

- Sample media release as a Word document for use as a template
- Mobile industry logo and links to more information

Resources

The following resources are included to help you with further research and/or implementation of the ideas found in this chapter.

Associations

Word of Mouth Marketing Association, www.womma.org

Free Reports

Blogging for Profits Blueprint, Yaro Starek,
  mobilemarketingprofits.com/243/blog-profits-blueprint
The New Rules of Viral Marketing: How Word-of-Mouse Spreads Your Ideas
  for Free, David Meerman Scott,
  www.davidmeermanscott.com/documents/Viral_Marketing.pdf
Online Video Marketing: Ten Ways You Can Use YouTube to Promote Your
  Online Content, tinyurl.com/videomktg

College Marketing Services

Alloy Media + Marketing, www.alloymarketing.com
Campus Media Group, www.campusmediagroup.com
CampusParty, www.campusclients.com

Blog Ad Networks

b5media, www.b5media.com/advertise
Blogads, www.blogads.com
Federated Media Publishing, www.federatedmedia.net
FeedBurner: Ads for Blogs and Feeds,
  www.feedburner.com/fb/a/advertising

Pay-per-Click Advertising

Google AdWords, adwords.google.com
Yahoo! Search Engine Marketing, searchmarketing.yahoo.com
MSN's Microsoft adCenter, www.adcenter.microsoft.com

Books

David Meerman Scott, *The New Rules of Marketing and PR: How to Use News Releases, Blogs, Podcasting, Viral Marketing and Online Media to Reach Buyers Directly* (Wiley, 2007)

Publicity Firms

EMSI (Event Management Services, Inc.), www.emsincorporated.com
The Geek Factory, Inc., www.geekfactory.com
Hot Guest, www.hotguest.com

Media Release Distribution Outlets

Business Wire, www.businesswire.com
Press Kit 24/7, www.247presskit.com
PR Newswire, www.prnewswire.com
PRWeb, www.prweb.com

Media Lists

Bulldog Reporter's Media List Builder, listbuilder.bulldog reporter.com
Harrison's Guide to the Top National TV Talk and Interview Shows, www.nationaltvshows.com
Media Contacts Pro, www.mediacontactspro.com

CHAPTER

Tracking Your Results

It's not enough simply to measure how many visits you get to your mobile site; you need a deeper understanding of what those visitors are doing.

—Ray Anderson, CEO, Bango

The beauty of working with the Internet and now with mobile is that you can effectively track your campaigns from launch to sale. You can tell exactly what is working and what isn't. Thankfully, the days described by John Wanamaker, who said, "Half the money I spend on advertising is wasted; the trouble is I don't know which half," are long gone. With mobile, you can also track your other marketing as well. If you have a billboard campaign that is currently a brand awareness campaign (in which you are not requesting a specific response, only brand recognition), you may have no idea how well it is working. Are people driving by seeing it? Are they noticing your brand and your campaign? If you add an offer for a mobile coupon that is only shown on that billboard, you can now count exactly how many sales are direct results of that billboard. Sweet.

You can literally divide the cost of the billboard and the text message campaign by the number of sales. Was it worth the cost? You will know if it was. You will still accomplish your brand awareness as well. This results-oriented mechanism can be embedded through mobile marketing in almost any other marketing you do. You are tracking your mobile marketing campaign, and by tracking it, you are also getting input about your other marketing efforts.

You can get access to all this information using mobile site analytic software. With mobile web as with the Internet, you can track your visitors and find out where they came from and where they went after visiting your site. You can also learn other information about them, including where they are from, what handset they are using, what keywords they used to get to your site, who purchased anything from you, and what ad campaign they clicked on to get to your site.

With your mobile, you can even make sales from your advertising. Instead of using a marketing campaign and hoping your customers will go home and buy it online or come into your store, your customers can buy from you using their mobile devices. By integrating a mobile payment system such as PayPal Mobile or ShopText into your campaign, you can actually drive sales. (See Chapter 13 for details about mobile payment systems.) Using a mobile payment integrated system, a person could order a new CD from a billboard in the same time it takes for a traffic light to turn green. A customer who is standing in front of a sign about an upcoming event could send an affirmative RSVP and pay for his registration fee right there. Likewise, a public speaker could sign up audience members and have them paying for a premium text club before she has even finished speaking. A person riding a bus who is looking at the bus ads could buy tickets to a concert via a cell phone before getting off at the next stop. Whether you are counting sales, leads, or click-throughs, mobile can make almost any marketing responsive, letting you know exactly which half of your marketing campaign is working so you can stop investing in the half that isn't.

What to Track and How to Use the Results

Obviously, you first want to track your results: sales, coupon redemption, incoming calls, mobile website visitors, and whatever you set up your campaign to accomplish. Start by determining the process you will use to keep track of these results. If you are tracking and they are not online, you'll need a way to tie a physical sale to a campaign in your records. For a small one-location business, this could be simple. The person ringing up the sale can use a piece of paper and make tick marks to track sales for the day or the week. Perhaps a mobile coupon was redeemed and the storeowner created a special coupon code to use at the register. For larger businesses with hundreds of employees and dozens of locations, this won't work, and the process will have to be automated. Fortunately, a large business will already have a method in place to handle the tracking. For example, Redbox free movie Monday codes are simply an alphanumeric number sent in the text message and then input into the kiosk as a payment mechanism. The Borders mobile coupon offers also include a promotion code in the text, but the code is verbally given to cashiers at Borders to enter into the register.

With mobile marketing, intermediate points along the way can and should also be tracked. If you have a mobile website with a mobile ad campaign to drive traffic to your mobile site via a mobile coupon and redeem it, you can track the coupon redemption and how many people came to your site compared to the number of requests for the coupon. You can even track how many people saw the ad versus how many actually clicked on it. Each of these points along the marketing timeline gives you a chance to improve your results. For an example, I've used small numbers so it is easy to do and see the math. These are not intended as representative samples; these just explain the tracking methods. In the following charts, we are using a hypothetical campaign that consists of mobile advertising that leads to a mobile coupon opt-in page that we then track all the way through redemption.

Sample Campaign

Let's begin with a sample campaign:

Ad Impressions (people who see your ad on other mobile sites)	100,000
Ad Click-Through Rate (response rate your ad gets)	5 percent
Mobile Site Visitors (how many people see your coupon offer)	5,000
Coupon-Take Percent (response your coupon offer gets)	15 percent
Coupons Requested (how many people receive the coupon)	750
Coupons Redeemed (number of coupons used)	300
Redemption Stat (coupons redeemed divided by coupons requested)	40 percent
Average Sale Per Coupon (how much people spent when using the coupon)	$25
Total Sales	**$7,500**

If you take a closer look at these numbers, you'll see what tracking can do. If you can improve your ad and get 1,000 more people to click on it, your click-through rate (CTR) will jump from 5 percent to 6 percent, and you will increase your total sales by 20 percent. This does assume nothing else changes in the process. Improving your CTR gets more people to participate in your marketing campaign. Your CTR can be increased by changing the content of the ad (the graphic or the text), choosing different places to display the ads, or switching your ads to keep them fresh. On a mobile screen, ad blindness (when people just don't "see" the ad any more) sets in quickly. Keep an eye on the rest of your numbers; different sources of traffic often have different response rates.

Sample Campaign with Improved Click-Through Rate

Here's another sample campaign:

Ad Impressions	100,000
Ad Click-Through Rate (your improvements)	6 percent
Mobile Site Visitors (result is 1,000 more visitors)	6,000
Coupon-Take Percent	15 percent
Coupons Requested (gets 150 more coupons out)	900
Coupons Redeemed (60 more people redeem coupon)	360
Redemption Stat	40 percent
Average Sale Per Coupon	$25
Total Sales*	**$9,000**

*With no other changes, sales increased by 20 percent

Now let's say you improve the page where people are first offered the coupon and increase the number of people who take the coupon. This is known as improving your conversion. In this example, you are driving ad traffic to a landing page that offers a mobile coupon. In reality, it could be anything else you want people to do after they click on your ad: using a click-to-call to your business, providing an email address to opt in to your email list, or downloading something. At this stage, you are trying to get more people to accept or request your initial offer. In this case, it is the coupon. To do that, you can write different copy, change the way people accept the coupon, add a graphic, or even change the coupon offer. So if you make the coupon more appealing and get a 3 percent boost in your coupon-take response, you're now getting an 18 percent conversion rate from your mobile site. Here's what happens:

Sample Campaign with Improved Coupon Take

Ad Impressions	100,000
Ad Click-Through Rate	6 percent
Mobile Site Visitors	6,000
Coupon-Take Percent (your improvements)	18 percent
Coupons Requested (gets 180 more coupons out)	1,080
Coupons Redeemed (72 more people redeem the coupon)	432
Redemption Stat	40 percent
Average Sale Per Coupon	$25
Total Sales*	**$10,800**

*Another 20 percent increase in sales

The next step is increasing the coupon redemptions. Perhaps you can make it easier for people to redeem the coupons or make the offer easier to understand. You could even change the offer entirely. Maybe a Buy-One-Get-One-Free offer is more appealing to your customers than 25 percent off the entire order. Or maybe giving people a shorter time frame to use the coupon will give you a better redemption rate. Perhaps, if you made it clear up front that your customers would receive a coupon and a message, you can remind people when a coupon is about to expire. This would be a good deal if these reminders increased the redemption rate more than offering actually decreased the coupon request rate. It's only through tracking and analysis that you know what works and what doesn't. If you don't know your coupon redemption rate to begin with, then how will you know if changing something actually makes it better? Let's see what happens in our hypothetical example if the coupon redemption increased by 6 percent:

Sample Campaign with Improved Coupon Redemption

Ad Impressions	100,000
Ad Click-Through Rate	6 percent
Mobile Site Visitors	6,000
Coupon-Take Percent	18 percent
Coupons Requested	1,080
Coupons Redeemed	486
Redemption Stat (your improvements)	45 percent
Average Sale Per Coupon	$25
Total Sales*	**$12,150**

*Sales increased another 12.5 percent for a total of 62 percent.

In this example, you can see how tracking your campaign and taking action to improve it at each stage can increase your sales by 62 percent. This is the power of tracking. By tracking each step of your campaign from the initial contact with a customer to the actual sale, you have quantifiable, objective ways to decide what you need to change to improve your campaign. If all you know is how much you spend on mobile advertising and what your total sales are, you are missing several opportunities to make the campaign more successful. If your CTR on the ad is too low, the rest of the campaign will suffer. If your coupon take percentage is low, and you know it because you're tracking it, you can devote your time to getting a higher redemption. Or perhaps you are getting a high CTR (plenty of traffic going to the site), but you're not getting a high enough conversion. These numbers provide focus and strategic information about what details you need to work on to improve your campaign. If you are involved in mobile marketing and you're not tracking your results, you are losing out on a great opportunity to boost your sales.

How to Track Your Campaign

At each step of your mobile campaign, you have the ability to track how well each specific stage of your campaign is working. You'll use a range of different tools to determine your campaign success, and it will be up to you to pull them all together for an overall analysis. Stay on top of your campaign, and use the analysis of it to reap the rewards of a bigger return on your investment.

Advertising Click-Through Rates

When you launch a mobile ad campaign with companies such as AdMob, JumpTap, Google, or Medio, they will provide the tracking tools for the CTR on your ads. Pay close attention to these numbers right from the start. The first click is the start to the entire campaign, and the more successful your ad is, the more successful your campaign will be. So become familiar with your ad campaign dashboard. It is likely to give you more information than you know how to use. Be sure to enlist your ad network account representatives for help, since they work on many campaigns and have a wealth of knowledge. Ask them for advice on your campaigns because the more click-throughs you get, the more money they make too. In Chapter 10, an entire section is devoted to mobile advertising and how to run the best campaign possible.

Split Testing

To get the best possible ad CTR, you need to run split tests, which is simply comparing two different ads to see which one gets the best response. You are comparing the response that Ad A gets to the response from Ad B. If possible, let your ad campaign software provide the results. Google AdWords has been doing this for years. You'll need to create two ads, and let them run long enough to get impressions. One of the ads will likely be doing better than the other. Keep the more successful ad running and try another ad against that one. Again, one of them will be getting a better response. Keep that one and repeat the process throughout the entire campaign. You never know when you will discover the magic formula with the best appeal for your customers. The details of split testing could fill an entire book or seminar, and I recommend further reading about it. It will be worth it because, as shown in the example campaign, each phase of the campaign that can be done better has a direct impact on the bottom line.

Here's one tool worth checking out: SplitTester.com (www.split tester.com). What you will find on this simple site, created by Perry Marshall and Bryan Teasley, is a quick form to fill out with the results from two ads. Simply input how many clicks you received and what the CTR was for each ad. After you fill in the information, click on the Calculate button to see whether you have a statistical winner. Sometimes just comparing the CTR percentages is not enough. This free tool will tell you whether you have a valid split-test result.

Mobile Web Analytics

The same website tracking tools that work on the desktop Internet do not work on the mobile web. The technology is just not the same. Browser-based techniques such as cookies and Java scripts don't work on mobile so the analysis is not accurate for a mobile site. Instead, you need a mobile web analytical software package that will track detailed information and analytics, including what specific handset your visitor is using, what carrier that phone is on, and the specific capabilities for each phone. Your analytical software can tell you how often your return visitors change phones and what kinds of other sites your visitors frequent. It is amazing to see the amount of usable information you can get via mobile analytical software. Some effective and affordable mobile-specific analytical software is available to track all statistics related to your mobile site, even at this early stage of mobile marketing. See the Resources section at the end of this chapter for a list of options.

Knowing these key pieces of information about your visitors can help you develop more targeted and robust campaigns. For example, if you want to know what percentage of your visitors support streaming video, download MP3 files frequently, or visit a particular genre of other mobile sites, your mobile analytic software can provide the answers. If you want to know the most common screen size that your visitors are using, you can find that out too. More importantly, certain mobile analytical software tools can show you exactly where your advertising dollars are going. Mobilytics, one of the mobile analytic packages, can help create tracking URLs to use in all your ads. You can track each ad by campaign, by ad network, and by keyword, and then describe exactly what you are getting for your ad dollars. If you are paying for ads that search engine crawlers or desktop computer users click on, you will know. You can then even tie these ad campaigns directly to sales made on your mobile and get an exact amount of revenue per ad.

Using Analysis to Make Changes on Your Mobile Site

Setting up the data analysis for your mobile campaign is just the first step. You need to take action based on that analysis. Here is an example of data that is found and what action can be taken to improve your campaign.

One thing we struggle with on the mobile web is forms. Let's say we have a lead generation form that asks for an email address. While filling out that form would be considered a "Goal" with an overall conversion rate, that rate needs to be looked at deeper. Let's say overall conversion rate for the lead form is 1.07%.

As an analyst, you naturally ask yourself how you can increase that. Well on the wired web, the changes that you make will affect all visitors in the same way. Every computer has a screen, mouse and keyboard. Other than screen size, we're not talking much difference. With mobile analytics, you need to look deeper. The overall conversion rate might be 1.07%, but what is the conversion rate for those visitors that have QWERTY keyboards? So we take a look and we see that number jump to 3.23%!

Well that tells us something, doesn't it? If everyone had a QWERTY keyboard, the conversion rate would be much higher. So what can you do? Well that's up to you. Maybe you break the email address into two text boxes with the "@" between them so users don't need to find that symbol. Maybe you use one text box, an "@" and a drop down of the most popular domain extensions. What's great about analytics is you can make the change and know quickly if it increases the conversion.

—Greg Harris, www.mobilewebanalytics.net

Of course, having all the data in the world doesn't do any good if you don't use it. You need to check in on your data regularly, make decisions, and take action based on what you learn. The more you do this, the easier it will become. Keep detailed notes of your strategy and the data you based it on. If you changed your product offering based on the most commonly used devices by your audience, then make sure that device is the one most commonly used. If that changes, you'll need to refocus and take new action. The key to effective campaign tracking is to respond to the data you have gathered.

Chapter Updates and Online Resource Guide

Updates to this chapter and its related Online Resource Guide are available at www.mobilemarketinghandbook.com/Updates/Tracking.

The Online Resource Guide for Chapter 6 includes links for all sites listed in this chapter, as well as a detailed review of web-analytic software choices.

Resources

The following resources are included to help you with further research and/or implementation of the ideas found in this chapter.

Web-Analytic Software Choices

AdMob Mobile Analytics, www.admob.com
Amtheon Solutions,
    www.amethon.com/Content_Common/pg-Mobile-Analytics.seo
Bango Analytics,
    www.mobilemarketingprofits.com/reviews/bango-analytics
GetMobile Analytics, www.getmobile.com
Mobilytics, www.mobilytics.net

Books

Perry Marshall and Bryan Todd, *Ultimate Guide to Google Adwords*
    (Entrepreneur Press, 2006)

Research Sources and Companies

AdMob Mobile Metrics—Free Report, www.admob.com/metrics
eMarketer, www.emarketer.com
Juniper Research, www.juniperresearch.com
M:Metrics, www.mmetrics.com
Mobile Marketing Association, www.mmaglobal.com

P A R T

Mobile Marketing Toolbox: Tactics, Campaign Ideas, and Resources

If you are ready to start a mobile marketing campaign, Part 2 will guide you through each of the tactics you can use. Voice, text messaging, and mobile advertising can be quickly and easily implemented, and, for the most part, the general public is ready to jump aboard when you do.

Other tactics, such as location-based marketing, mobile social networking, and marketing with audio or video, are not as easy to launch. These tactics are not quite as straightforward, and, in some cases, the tools needed to implement an effective campaign are not yet available. Often, enough consumers are just not up to speed with the technology for a viable campaign to be launched.

To help you determine which mobile marketing approach you should use right now, Part 2 is organized in order of each tactic's ability to be implemented in terms of the software and vendor support as well as the openness of consumers to use their mobile devices in the fashion you require. Since getting people to make calls with their mobile phones has no technological barriers and 100 percent of mobile users use the phone call feature on their phones, the first chapter in this section covers voice. Then you'll find chapters on text messaging, the mobile web, and mobile web promotion strategies of search, advertising, and publicity that are all fairly accessible and have ample support. A chapter on mobile social networking, which many industry insiders claim will be the next big thing, follows; however, there are not always clear-cut ways to use it for marketing purposes.

Coverage on proximity marketing appears near the end of Part 2 because it is a more complicated approach and more likely to take time for consumers to adapt to engaging with businesses based on their locations. The final chapter covers tools and techniques that don't require a full chapter by themselves. Don't miss this one since there are some important topics, including widgets and iPhone application development, mobile payment options, and mobile email.

Voice

Voice is still the killer application. As an agency, we use voice because it has the largest audience and has the ability to enter-tain, engage and inspire in ways that text messaging can't.
—Gene Keenan, Vice President of
mobile strategy for Isobar

What Is Voice?

Voice as a mobile marketing tool is exactly what you think it is: Someone makes a call with a mobile phone and interacts on the phone via voice. This can be a person-to-person call, a person-to-computer call, or even a person-to-recording phone call. It may seem quite low-tech and ordinary, but is it a powerful mobile marketing tool?

Yes. In fact, it is powerful because it is low-tech compared to other tools you can use. Anyone with a mobile phone can interact with your business using this method, even the "I-only-use-my-phone-for-calls" person. The people who don't have text message or data plans that let them jump onto the mobile web at moment's notice will appreciate marketing techniques that cater to them in a way they actually understand. And the folks who have high-tech features, such as text messaging or access to the mobile web, still can make phone calls with a mobile phone.

While voice may seem too basic to you, think about it as a potent mar-keting tool. There are plenty of ways to use voice in mobile marketing that will be attractive to your customers and give you a quick and easy way to get started with mobile. Some advanced techniques in the voice category inte-grate mobile web access and click-to-call. So don't dismiss this as a tool to be used only with a low-tech audience.

When to Use Voice as a Marketing Tool

If your audience is not tech-savvy (as determined by the Mobile-Savvy Worksheet in Chapter 1), voice is an ideal way to start a mobile marketing campaign. You can market to your customers via mobile. Just use your ad to tell them to call you "using your mobile phone right now." Yes, use words just like that. People need to have the plan of action that is clearly presented to them because they are busy. Tell them what to do when they want to take action after seeing your marketing. If you suggest using mobile as a way your customers can interact with you, you are essentially training your customers to use mobile.

Using voice as a mobile marketing tool also works well when you have one-way communication to share that takes more than 160 characters (the limit for text messaging), and your customers want the information quickly (no time to log on to the mobile web). For example, think about using this tool for directions to your place of business or when you want to share more detailed information about a specific promotion. Your customers can grab their phones, dial your number, and get what they need right now. Voice also works well for an extensive, interactive discussion with your customers. Getting your customers to call you is still often the best call-to-action you can choose. When encouraging incoming phone calls is the right thing for your business (you'll know it), go for it.

How to Use Voice: Best Practices, Tips, and Techniques

To use voice, simply tell people how and why they should call you and then suggest that they do it right now with their mobile phones. Obviously, this is done via a marketing campaign that your customers will encounter while they are mobile. This is not part of your Yellow Pages ad, TV advertising, or direct mail, as it would seem odd to suggest that they use their mobile phones to call you when their landline phone is handy. Instead, you would use this in radio ads, signage, out-of-home TV advertising, and event marketing that your customers see and hear when they are out of the house with their trusty cell phones at their sides.

Your marketing strategy needs to convey a sense of urgency to make this work. Your customers should feel they need to call now or they will miss out on something. Don't go overboard, but don't miss this crucial component either. If they don't call right now via their mobile phones, they probably won't remember to call later. Plus, they are unlikely to have the number handy at that time. The bigger the reason you give them to call now, the better.

The best practices and legal implications associated with this type of marketing are insignificant. You won't need to educate people about calling or warn them that using their cell phone minutes can potentially cost them money. They already know this. The important part of this strategy is to compel them to call you. This is true of all marketing. The reason someone should come to your business must be spelled out clearly so that your customers want to take action. Without a reason to participate, people simply won't do it.

Incoming Calls to Your Business

The most basic way to get customers to act on your marketing is for them to call your business. To make sure this happens, include your phone number in your marketing and ask your audience to call you. Be simple and straightforward. When customers call, they initially reach your receptionist, front desk, reservation department, subscription department, sales, booking team, or the person who usually handles incoming calls. If you want to (and you should), track how many incoming calls result from your marketing targeted specifically to mobile users. You can use a certain phone number just for those calls. That way, you can easily track your marketing campaign without adding more work for your staff. When you get people to call your business from your other marketing ads and signs, be sure to include a phone number for them to respond. In this case, the mobile phone is a direct response tool and nothing more. But don't be put off by this simplicity. Cell phone users know how to make a call with their phones, but the same cannot be said for other functions, including text messaging, going onto the mobile web, using social networking, or watching video. The key to making this work is in the marketing that drives the call. That's where you need to think creatively.

Think outside the box: Come up with several places where your customers have their mobile phones with them and where they can call you easily at the time they want to call. Then, you will have laid the foundation for a good mobile marketing campaign.

Pay-per-Call

Pay-per-call is a form of online advertising where your business and phone number is advertised, but you only pay when someone actually calls your business. It is almost the same as pay-per-click, but the action is different. The ads are placed online in search engines such as Google, Yahoo!, MSN, Local, and online Yellow Pages. These online ads are also placed in mobile search engines such as AOL Mobile, MSN Mobile, and JumpTap (this search engine powers many mobile carriers on desk search engines). Your pay-per-call ads are also provided via directory assistance such as 1-800-FREE-411 and 1-800-411-SAVE. Pay-per-call is a powerful way to get calls coming into your business, and you only pay when the advertising works. This option is always free for customers.

Pay-per-call is an effective tool to use with mobile marketing. It is the perfect direct response mechanism of a mobile search if you want your prospective customers to call you. And instead of your customers searching on their phones through mobile websites to get what they want, let them connect to you instantly on their phones with the exact device they are using to find you. The following is the basic process of a pay-per-call campaign:

- Write a brief description of your business and the services you offer. Be as descriptive as possible and put in the most prominent information first. You never know how much of your pay-per-call listing will appear on someone's phone.

- Determine the geographic area where you want your ad to appear when someone searches. You can appear nationally, regionally, or locally.

- Figure out the categories that best describe your business. You can choose from broad categories to specific ones. The more specific you get, the fewer times your ad will actually appear. However, your reach will be that much more targeted to your audience.

- Decide the maximum price you are willing to pay for a lead, or a call made to you as a result of seeing your ad. Take some time to calculate this figure; if you don't already know your revenue-per-customer (how much you earn from each new customer), then figure it out. The key is to pay less for the lead than you will earn from a new customer. And remember that all the calls you receive may not be from new customers; you may receive calls from current customers too.

- Set up your pay-per-call campaign. This is an easy, do-it-yourself online campaign. See the Resources section at the end of this chapter for vendors who offer this service.

- Wait for the phone to ring. (You won't hear me say that often.)

- Track how well your campaign is working. You need to know how often these incoming calls turn into actual customers as well as the number of returning customers. If the number of current customers who are calling you this way is higher than you are willing to pay for, then it means you're not easy enough to find another way. You can launch a customer service campaign where you inundate your customers with your phone number as well as beef up your mobile search engine marketing so you are more easily found when someone is looking for your number.

Click-to-Call

Click-to-call (a link on a mobile web page that when clicked initiates a phone call) works the way pay-per-call does except there are no fees involved. Usually, it's an option on your own mobile website to make it easier for your visitors to call you. You simply format the phone number using your mobile website building tool to turn on the click-to-call feature. It can be used with mobile ad campaigns that drive traffic to a page that gives people the option of calling you. But neither you nor your customers are charged for the call.

Redbook magazine does this on its mobile site (m.redbook mag.com). The navigation on every page includes a link to "Subscribe." By clicking this link, the mobile site visitor is prompted to "CLICK TO CALL toll-free 1-877-273-2322" to sign up for a subscription to the magazine. This is one example of starting a call-to-action with click-to-call. Not only does it say that it is click-to-call and is a clickable link, but the phone number is also displayed just in case the user's phone doesn't work when he clicks on the link. The customers can still easily call to get their subscriptions.

Call a Recording

Another way to market to your customers is with a recorded message when they call. Granted, this is simple voice mail technology, but if you use your creativity and think about where your customers are spending time waiting (and have their mobile phones with them), you can get them to call your voice mail and listen to a recording. Before you have them call your number to listen to a commercial, remember that no one participates just to hear or see the commercials, unless it is during the Super Bowl. Your recording has to include some entertaining, informative, or helpful element.

For example, if an amusement park posts a sign in the busy queue area where people are waiting for a ride, the visitors waiting in line would see a sign with a phone number to call. They can then listen to a recording with trivia, a visual scavenger hunt (think "I Spy" via voice mail), or a quick story. At the end of the recording, the park can include a prompt to send a text message to get a coupon for a caramel apple, a T-shirt, or another money-making item. This way, the people who are waiting are entertained, and the day at the park is more fun for them. The amusement park also gets to engage its visitors in a new way by getting them to request a coupon that encourages more spending inside the park. If you have customers waiting in line for your services, you can consider trying this marketing technique.

Think where people in your target market are waiting for something and advertise there too. A restaurant near an automotive service shop can advertise a two-minute voice recording of "Five Ideas for Dinner Tonight." Four of them can be quick, make-at-home dinner ideas, and the fifth can suggest stopping at the nearby restaurant. Offer a coupon via mobile so you can track how well this works. Instead of having your customers waiting around in boredom, you can entertain them and attract new ones through smart mobile marketing.

Abbreviated Dialing Codes

An outstanding opportunity for major brands or companies with a major budget is a technology called abbreviated dialing codes (ADCs). These are a three- to six-digit alpha numeric code preceded by a # sign: BET (#BET), Univision (#323), MTV (#MTV), Fox News (#3696), and Sears (#SEARS). When mobile users dial such a number sequence into their phones, it makes a call for them. The call is answered by a computerized voice giving easy-to-follow prompts such as "Press 1 for this" and "Press 2 for that," or the phone will immediately begin downloading a ringtone, playing a broadcast, or connecting callers to live customer service representatives. ADC campaigns are similar to text message campaigns in pricing, carrier approval, and the time frame it takes to launch a campaign; these are described in detail in Chapter 8.

Chapter Updates and Online Resource Guide

Updates to this chapter and its related Online Resource Guide are available at www.mobilemarketinghhhandbook.com/Updates/Voice.

The Online Resource Guide for Chapter 7 includes links for all sites listed in this chapter.

Resources

The following resources are included to help you with further research and/or implementation of the ideas found in this chapter.

Pay-per-Call

Ingenio, www.ingenio.com

Abbreviated Dialing Codes

SingleTouch, www.singletouch.net

CHAPTER

Text Message Campaigns

*SMS texting is used by 2 billion people, about twice as many peo-
ple send SMS text messages as use any other messaging types
combined including email and instant messaging. SMS texting
is the nearest thing to a universal format for media content on
the mobile phone.*

—Tomi T Ahonen

What Is Text Messaging?

Text messaging, also known as texting, is the process of sending a short
message using a maximum of 160 characters to a cell phone via short message service (SMS). The majority of text messages are sent from one cell
phone directly to another as a form of personal communication. Text messages can also be sent commercially via text message services that send
texts to multiple phones simultaneously. It is that commercial form of text
messaging that is covered in this chapter.

When to Use Text Messaging as a Marketing Tool

My recommendation is that if you want to do any mobile marketing, start
with a text messaging effort, especially if your customers are a mobile-
savvy audience as described in Chapter 1.

Text message campaigns are the easiest and most affordable mobile
marketing campaign to launch by far, and they are also the most likely to
succeed now. Text messaging is the easiest to implement because it is a universal application on cell phones and across carriers. Even basic cell
phones can do it, and it works the same on all phones, so the technological
barriers to launch a campaign are much lower than with any other mobile

marketing tool. The costs have become affordable for even small businesses. The reason a text message campaign is most likely to succeed is that more people send and receive text messages than use the mobile Internet or any other mobile application besides phone calling.

How to Use Text Messaging: Best Practices, Tips, and Techniques

As you know from previous chapters, mobile marketing only works if you have permission from the mobile user and that is especially true with text messaging. You can't buy a list of mobile phone numbers and start sending out messages. That would be text spam. Not only will the customers not buy from you, the Federal Trade Commission, your state attorney general, and the phone carriers will stop you in a hurry. Get permission first before sending an SMS or standard text message and work on the value proposition: What value are you providing to your customers? Once you answer that question, you can proceed.

Text Message Campaign Basics

The basic concept of text messaging in marketing is sending short (a maximum of 160 characters) messages in response to people who opt in to your text message campaign. You can entice customers or potential customers to participate; once they agree by sending a text message to you (or opting in on your website), then you send them a text message. You can use a variety of approaches, from contests (known as text-to-win), mobile coupons, text clubs/subscriptions, sending a link to a mobile site, voting/polling, alerts, or even sending out a blast to a group who agreed to be texted for a particular reason. I'll cover each of these techniques in detail in this chapter, but let's go over the basic tools of text messaging first.

Short Codes and Keywords

If you've watched an episode of *American Idol* or seen a message with words similar to "Text Tacos to 12345," you know what a short code is and what a keyword is. The five- to six-digit number (12345) is the short code, and the word that is texted (Tacos) is the keyword. You need to have a short code and a keyword (or maybe several) to proceed with a text messaging campaign. These are the basic tools to use in your campaign. Short codes can be vanity codes (where the numbers spell out a word to promote your brand), or they can be random numbers. In most instances, a random short code will work since your customer will most likely take immediate action using the short code and not need to remember it for long.

In a process that is similar to registering for a domain name, you must apply for a short code from the Common Short Code Administration (www.usshortcodes.com). This is where the similarity ends, because there is a six- to eight-week waiting period while your short code is assigned and while cell phone carriers approve your campaign. You will pay $500 to $1,000 per month in advance for the short code lease in 3-, 6- or 12-month increments. This lease will give your company exclusive rights to use the specific short code number you have acquired for the duration of your lease. If you have a specific need for a dedicated short code and the budget to do so, you should lease your own short code.

However, if you have a modest budget, have no need for a dedicated short code, or just want to get started faster, you can use a shared short code through a text message company. This means other companies will be marketing the same short code number, but you will have a unique keyword that will identify your campaign. Since the text message company that runs the shared short code already has its code provisioned, there is no waiting period, so you can sign up with a company and set up your first campaign within minutes. This is a huge advantage over leasing your own short code. In the time it takes a major brand to request and be approved for a texting campaign, you can launch your text message campaign and already have a few months of success under your belt. The fees are about $100 per month for shared access to the short code and the software to manage campaigns. Whether you lease your own short code or share one, you will also pay a per-message fee with discounts per message based on higher volume.

SMTP Messaging

Using a short code is the only viable way to run a commercial text message campaign. Technologically, you can send email messages to phones that appear to the receiver as if they are text messages. These are emails sent to the phone number at the carriers' email address using SMTP (simple mail transfer protocol) technology. Unlike SMS text messages, there is no charge for these messages to be sent, which is why this method of delivery seems appealing. However, SMTP messages are unreliable—often with one- to two-hour delays, and delivery is never guaranteed. Because these messages are not paid for, carriers don't have to deliver them so sometimes they do and sometimes they don't. Additionally, it is not possible for an automatic, one-step opt-out mechanism to be included so these messages are non-compliant with standard best practices. The risk of non-compliance is having all communications cut off from your SMTP server to phones on any network. And because an email address is used to deliver the message, all CAN-SPAM penalties apply. One complaint from a cell phone user could cost you up to $11,000 in fines. Lastly, this type of technology only works one way, so all types of campaigns that take advantage of two-way communication with your customers, including polling/voting or contests, are off the table. You may be tempted to use "free" message-sending capability, but in reality, the price of unreliability is enormous, and the risk of having a campaign shut down is not worth it. The bottom line is that using SMTP technology to run a text message campaign is not advised.

SMS Messaging

SMS is basic text messaging. The only charge to customers is whatever they pay for text messages to their cell phone companies. The charge to the business is for the software or services to run the campaign and for each text message. For the purposes of marketing your business, you will probably use SMS text messaging exclusively. It is the most consumer-friendly form of messaging because people are most familiar with how it works. Since there is no additional charge for your customers beyond their usual text message plan, it is the most affordable option for your customers.

Premium Messaging

Premium messaging is when customers pay a fee to send or get a text message. As an example, a person may pay 99 cents to cast a vote in a text message campaign. Or perhaps they pay $1.99 per month to receive a subscription to a set of text messages that are sent out regularly. A premium-messaging campaign is more complicated to start, but it can be a lucrative opportunity. However, it cannot be enacted using a shared short code so up-front costs are involved. This makes a premium campaign more complicated and definitely more expensive to get started. It is not likely you will use premium messages for marketing purposes because consumers don't typically pay to receive marketing.

Multimedia Messaging

Although it is similar to SMS, multimedia messaging (MMS) involves multimedia graphics. MMS was expected to take off as an effective mobile marketing tool, but MMS messages are not universally accepted or sent from all phones. This means that a sender has to know if the recipient can accept an

MMS before the message is sent. Additionally, the cost of sending and receiving MMS messages is higher because it uses a different technology to send the message. I don't advise using MMS campaigns for those reasons. If you must use multimedia, then it is better to use SMS to send a link to a mobile site to allow your customer to access the multimedia over the mobile web. Or you can use Bluetooth technology instead. See Chapter 12 for more on Bluetooth mobile zones and Chapter 9 for more about the mobile web.

How Many Mobile Industry Players Does It Take to Send a Text Message?

Sending a personal, one-to-one text message is simple. All you need to know is a phone number and that your intended recipient is text message-savvy with a text plan. In this case, one person uses one phone to send another person a text message to his phone. A commercial version of text messaging is more complicated and involves four or five types of companies working together to make it happen. But don't worry: Launching a text message campaign is easy.

Before you begin, it is helpful to know who you are working with along the way. First, as you can see in Figure 8.1, your company is the content provider. You are doing the promotion. If you choose, the next company to be involved is the advertising agency. If you are working with an agency, it will take care of every other company in this interaction for you. The agency is also responsible for the creative concepts and integration with your other marketing strategies. Since you will obviously not run a text message campaign using your personal cell phone, you need a company with the software to provide a short code and to send/receive the text messages for your campaign. These are called application providers within the mobile industry. In this book, I refer to them as text message companies because it is easier to remember. The text message companies (application providers) must then work with connection aggregators that provide the technical backbone by connecting the text message companies to the mobile carriers (cell phone companies). Although you won't work directly with connection aggregators, they are important because each aggregator has different agreements with different phone companies. Their service determines which cell phone companies your customers must subscribe to in order to participate in your campaign. (You have seen this when TV shows with interactive voting, such as *American Idol*, can only accept text message votes from people using certain wireless companies.) The last and most important connection in this

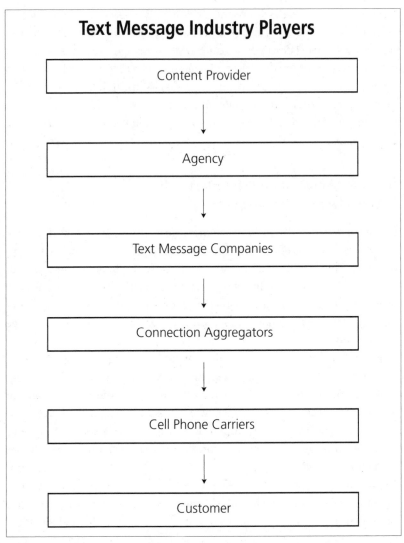

Text Message Industry Players

Content Provider

Agency

Text Message Companies

Connection Aggregators

Cell Phone Carriers

Customer

Figure 8.1   Sending short message service (SMS), or text messages, to cus-
tomers is not a direct path. This chart lists the many industry
players in the game.

entire process is with the cell phone companies, often referred to as carriers
(e.g., Sprint PCS, AT&T Wireless, T-Mobile, Verizon Wireless).

Again, you won't have any direct dealings with the cell phone carriers,
but they will have a huge impact on your campaign. Because carriers are
the ultimate provider of service to the end user, they must protect this relationship. If they let a smarmy spam campaign reach their subscribers, they

are likely to lose customers. Carriers can and do shut down (without notice) any and all campaigns that do not follow best practices. They also shut down campaigns for not producing adequate volume of messages. Even though you will have no direct dealings with them, the fate of your mobile marketing rests in the hands of the carriers. The best thing you can do to ensure a smooth working relationship with the carriers is to follow the industry best practices outlined in Chapter 3.

Four Text Messaging Best Practices

There are some best practices that are particularly important to text messaging. You'll want to follow all the industry guidelines, but these four are the most important.

The No. 1 best practice (and law) of text messaging is to get permission. Never send a text message that has not been explicitly requested. You will harm your business immeasurably if you do. Think permission, permission, permission. Have a crystal-clear opt-in process and always follow it. Your opt-in process includes the initial information offering the text messages. This will be your marketing for the campaign. Your customers will then sign up to receive your text messages. They will do this by texting your keyword to your short code or by using an Internet-based sign up form, called a widget. In order to build your list of text message recipients, you must actually launch a campaign. You cannot gather names and cell phone numbers and expect to import them into a program. Most text message companies will not let you import cell phone numbers into their database unless they come from another verifiable opt-in source. As an example, if you have a collection of customers' cell phone numbers in your customer contact database, you cannot simply begin to text message them. They must initiate the interaction via their cells or on the web to unequivocally request text messages from your company.

The second best practice of text messaging is honesty. Always tell your customers up front if they are going to be getting a subscription (more than one message). If you plan to send them more than the initial text message requested, then you are starting a subscription (even if you're sending free messages). Be clear how frequently you will contact them and if you are charging them for this service; tell them what the price and billing terms are. Don't imply that a service or subscription is free if it isn't. For example, don't say that they get free ringtones if they actually have to buy 10 at full price first.

The third best practice of text messaging is to provide people an easy way to opt out. Share this information in every message you send and in your Help message. The most commonly used approach is to tell your customers to send the words Stop or Remove to your short code. If you are using a shared short code, the opt-out text will be automatically inserted into each outgoing message for you. It will reduce the number of characters you can use for marketing to 140, but you don't have to remember to include the opt-out. Keep in mind that violating any of these rules can cause your campaign to be turned off without notice by the cell phone carriers. This is one of the most important reasons not to use SMTP for a messaging campaign: You cannot receive messages back in reply. Your only option for having an opt-out process involves using a website link, which is not in compliance with best practices.

As we investigate the options available in text messaging, it may be tempting to create a complex, multifaceted campaign. As the fourth best practice, keep it simple. Ask for one call-to-action for one specific purpose. Keep the actions that your customers need to do to the bare minimum. You want to keep it simple and straightforward so it is easy for your customer to participate. After all, the beauty of text messaging is ease of use and simplicity. Don't make your campaign too complicated; you could lose your audience.

Types of Text Message Campaigns

With the range of text message options available, the more creative you are in strategizing your campaign, the more attractive your campaign will be for your customers. If you can entice people to participate in the first place, you are more likely to be happy with your results. As you create mailing lists for your catalog, mailed newsletter, weekly flyer, and email campaigns, you also want to build your text message list. Start with this as quickly as you can. As I have noted previously, you cannot buy a list of cell phone numbers and send unsolicited text messages. Instead, you must entice your current and potential customers to give you their cell phone numbers in exchange for something that is of value to them. Do this within a working text message campaign that they opt into from their cell phones or online. This is the first step in your mobile marketing campaign. Build your list via a campaign. Following are some options for text message campaigns.

Text Club/Subscription

A text club/subscription is a series of text messages that your customers agree to receive on their phones. These can be either SMS messages or premium messages. It may be a weekly message, a Tuesday/Friday delivery, or a set number of messages per month. In some cases, people will want to sign up for daily texts. As long as you tell them you are sending a series, you can continue to send them messages. This is an important part of your planning. If you tell your mobile vendor that you only want a one-time contact campaign and set it up accordingly, then you can't return later and start contacting these people again. It is not within the best practices guidelines. If you intend to send out multiple messages, start your campaign by saying so.

A text club can be used in any of the following ways:

- Your m-zine – This is similar to an ezine, but instead of being sent via email, it is sent via mobile with plenty of useful content that can still fit into a 160-character limit. (To sign up for my mobile marketing m-zine, text KIMDUSHINSKI to 95495.)

- Joke/trivia of the day – Any tidbit of information can be shared as a text club.

- Quotes/inspiration – People may want to receive inspirational messages regularly.

- Greetings – A message from you that people will want to get.

- Product/service info – If you have a product or service that requires or could use regular communication, you can offer this as a text club.

Mobile Coupons

Mobile coupons are text message offers that are redeemable by having the customers show the text message at checkout time or submit a promotion code that was received via text. Mobile coupons are a perfect way to increase sales from your current customers, attract new customers, and promote loyalty. Mobile coupons are also ultimately trackable, so you can tell exactly how well your campaign worked. They are also the perfect tools for turning any of your other marketing efforts into a direct response tool. A simple billboard or sign can include an interactive call-to-action that drives trackable sales to your door. Any advertisement can incorporate this powerful response mechanism and dramatically increase the response rate of that ad.

The first step to starting a mobile coupon campaign is deciding whether you are offering a one-time deal or a series of discounts. You need to know this to set up your campaign and to create your marketing. One-time offers are likely to get a higher opt-in rate with new customers because people know they are only getting one message. But if you are marketing to current customers who already know and trust your brand, they may appreciate getting regular discounts. You can offer a one-time coupon, get people in the door the first time, and then get them to sign up for a text club or a coupon club.

The next step is to figure out what the "mobile" component is in your campaign. Why do your customers need to get your coupon on their phones? Is it that you tell them how to get the coupon when they are mobile, maybe while they are sitting on a bus, in their car at a stoplight, wandering around at a festival, or walking down the street? Or maybe you just want them to have the coupon with them when they are out and about, and they sign up for the coupon from the comfort of their computers. The better you do with aligning the mobile factor to your customers' wants and needs, the better response you will get from your mobile coupon. Keep in mind that as long as mobile coupons are new, your customers will be wondering how to redeem them. Include this education in your initial marketing to overcome any resistance they may have toward mobile coupons.

The following are some ideas for mobile coupons:

- Free trial offer – Get customers in the door to try your product or service. The beauty of the coupon being mobile is that they will have it with them when they are near your place of business.

- Special price or discount – New and current customers appreciate a special offer.

- Regular coupons – If you have people on a mobile list who have agreed to get coupons regularly, you can send a coupon for "10 percent off" on a particular day or just for certain products. You could have "Free Item Tuesdays" or "Bring a Friend for 25% off."

- Contest coupons – The first 50 people to respond to the ad are eligible for a free dessert with their meals or everyone will get free beverages. This combination limited offer (only the first 50 to respond) and coupon makes the offer more fun for the customers.

- Creative coupons – If your clientele would appreciate something quirky, try offering a limited-time coupon that is valid only if the person is wearing a certain color when they come in to redeem the coupon. "Come in by 5 PM wearing something green and receive a 2-for-1 dinner." This makes it more fun for the customers, too. Once they glance around the restaurant, they can see everyone else who is wearing green and see who likely came in because of the special offer.

Operational/Experience Messages

All text messages do not have to be sent with a sales goal in mind. In fact, many of the best text messaging opportunities rest in helping your customers with their experiences with your company. Chris Torbit from Blast Companies, who is a big advocate of these messages, is the one who shared the name for these with me. Calling them "reminder texts" just didn't work once I started thinking about the possibilities for experience messages. The idea is that communicating with your customers is important. The more avenues you have open for reaching your customers and for them to reach you, the better. As consumers become more tech-savvy, they will expect more access via technology to your company.

Check out the following examples:

- A delivery company can offer to send a text message when the driver is on the way and then send a customer service poll after the delivery.

- The dry cleaner can send a text message to let customers know their clothes are ready for pick up.

- An online retail store can send a "Your items have shipped" text message so the customer doesn't have to log into email.

- Businesses with customers who use text messaging frequently can be open to receiving customer service requests via text message.

Text-to-Mobile Site Link

With a text message, you can send a link to a mobile website, which is commonly called WAP push in the industry. After receiving a text message, your customer can click on the link and then connect to the Internet and directly to your mobile site. By using a simple tool (text message), you have the advantage of getting people to interact with your more complex marketing (mobile website). With this type of campaign, you can send people a link to a downloadable picture, video, ringtone, or audio message. Anything you can offer on the mobile web can be accessed via a link in a text message.

This technique saves time for your users. Not requiring your customers to type in the URL on their mobiles can be a big benefit, especially if they don't have a full QWERTY keyboard. I suggest sending a text message with a link only when you can't get enough information into a text message, or if there is another valid reason for taking your customers away from text and into the mobile web. Or maybe the reason for offering the text message is to drive traffic to a mobile website. When you send users to a fully interactive mobile website, be sure to tell them what they will get when they go there. People are busy; they don't have the time, energy, or interest to go to a mobile site unless they know how they will benefit. Provide value all the way through the process.

Here's an example of what a text-to-mobile-site text message might say:

> Check out XYZ's mobile website. Click here on your phone: http://m.xyzcompany.com. See times, get directions, find a map, coupons, and more.

One word of caution, though: Until it is common for your target market to click into mobile websites from text messages, educate your consumers when using this marketing technique. I learned this lesson from personal experience. Shortly after I bought my Treo and signed up for a data plan, the TV show *The Amazing Race* was promoting a text campaign where viewers could text the show and get back a list of the music that their favorite racing team listened to while racing around the world. It sounded like fun, and I expected to get a text message back with a couple of song titles in it. But when I sent my text, I received a simple message that said to go online to find out what my favorite team listened to while racing. A link was included in the text message, but it never occurred to me to click the link and look on my phone. I thought I was supposed to get up, go to my desktop computer, and go online while I was watching the show. Of course, I didn't click on the link on my phone, and I thought it was a stupid campaign. Months later, I realized the show was using this text-to-mobile site link technique. You can laugh at me now, but until users start going online regularly on a mobile device, many of your customers will have the same reaction I did. Include wording in your text message that lets people know it is a mobile site (see the sample later in this section). You can also specify in the marketing leading up to the customer's first action that they will be getting a link to a mobile site. For me, the commercial about sending a text message to *The Amazing Race* should have included the fact that I would get a link to the list of songs located on a mobile website.

Text Message Campaign Example

Let's say your restaurant is trying to get more repeat lunch business on Tuesdays. You already have a table top sign on every table that announces the weekly lunch specials each day. What if you design a way for people to use their mobile phones to vote for their favorite lunch special for the upcoming Tuesday. (They're just sitting there waiting to get their food anyway, so why not keep them entertained and engaged?)

On the next Tuesday morning, you can announce via a text message to all who voted which lunch special was selected. If a customer's entry won, how likely do you think that customer would be to come in to get it for lunch? You can even include a coupon in the text to provide further incentive and track your results.

Text Message Voting

Text message voting is quite popular for a good reason. First, it is easy and fun for customers, and second, it gives you valuable information about your customers. Here's how it works: Ask your customers a question, and they can answer (vote) using text messaging. You can ask the question anywhere your customers will see or hear it. You can ask them anything that they are likely to *want* to respond to (remember to provide value in this interaction or the campaign won't work). When they reply, your software will tally the votes. You can announce the winning response to all who voted (via a text message) and to your customers (via the same way you announced the original question).

The following examples offer some voting ideas:

- Radio stations or nightclub DJs can let listeners choose the next song by text vote. You can combine the vote with a contest so that the 10th text message received wins a prize or free drink. This can also work for talk radio stations that collect votes on a topic. Do you agree with Caller A or Caller B?

- Radio shows with more than one DJ can sponsor a contest where the audience decides who wins a bet between the DJs.

- Restaurants can let customers vote for their favorite desserts or specials. A follow-up coupon can be sent for the item for which they voted.

- Museums can offer a contest where customers can text message their votes about which exhibits are their favorites.

- A professional sports team can ask fans to vote for the game MVP or the Play of the Game.

- A professional speaker or professor can take a text message poll from the podium and announce the results from the stage.

Contests/Text-to-Win

People love winning things, and it is technologically easy to set up a contest or a text-to-win campaign. You can give away something small or huge as long as it is attractive enough to your customers to entice them to participate. In my first mobile marketing workshop, I included a contest for the folks who attended to win a copy of this book when it was published. It worked well, people were excited to win, and I told them that those who didn't win would be put on a mobile list to receive an announcement when the book was published. You can limit the contest to one-entry-per-phone, or you can let people vote multiple times. You can set up your odds to have more or fewer winners. If you're giving away a small ticket item, you can set up the odds for a 1 to 10 chance; if you are giving away a big item (such as an iTouch, digital camera, or car), you can set your odds higher. Text-to-win contests are an ideal way to get started with text campaigns because people love to win. Think creatively and design the perfect contest. But be sure to check out Chapter 3, Legal Issues and Implications of Mobile Marketing, before you create a sweepstakes or contest.

The following examples are some text-to-win contest ideas:

- An entertainer or band sponsors a contest on stage for fans to win a free CD/book.

- Fans at a sporting event try to win free hats or T-shirts.

- People at a crowded festival or street fair on a hot summer day text-to-win a seat inside an air-conditioned restaurant for an hour.

- Movie-theater patrons text-to-win free popcorn at the next movie they attend.

- A nightclub selects random patrons to win "no cover" entry if they send a text while waiting in line.

Text-to-Donate

For a charity event, you can arrange for people to text their donations via PayPal or another mobile payment provider. Because contributing this way is so easy, it can dramatically increase your donations. With one quick text message, people can send in a credit card donation, and you can eliminate staff to manage the donations and send the money to the charity instantly. This strategy works for radio stations during marathon charity drives, at large events such as rallies and walk-a-thons, and even non-charity events such as sporting events, concerts, festivals, and school gatherings where donations can be made. But you need to coordinate a mobile payment option, which is getting easier and easier. See the section on "Mobile Billing and Payment Options " in Chapter 13 for information on setting up such an option.

Text Alerts

People find timely knowledge valuable, and they are willing to sign up for alerts. Whatever timely alerts you can offer customers are likely to be welcome. Think of what alerts your customers need when they are mobile. Usually you can group these alerts into one of the following categories: pricing, availability, readiness, or emergency. Pricing is all about cost savings by alerting customers when they can save or when they need to shop before prices go up. Availability can range from an open table at a restaurant to an open chair in a styling salon or certain products on a limited basis. Collectors' items or the hot item at Christmas are good choices. Readiness is perfect when you offer a product or service that customers need to pick up or have delivered. Emergency alerts provide announcements to everyone in a certain area (think college campus, apartment complex, neighborhood, or office building) in which an emergency is taking place.

Text Message Campaign Tools

As you create and work with your SMS campaign, there will be times when you want to be more creative and interactive than what we've discussed. Other options exist for making your campaign more complex or using other tools with it.

Email Forwarding

Did you know that you don't have to receive incoming text messages on a website or on a phone? You can also have text messages sent to an email address. This works for campaign participants who are likely to be mobile while the recipient is likely to be at a computer with email access. Radio stations are a good example. People listen to the radio in their cars, and DJs are in the studio with a computer in front of them. Since they are already getting and reading emails from listeners, it doesn't change their processes at all, but it gives people more access to communicate. This is also an option for any business that wants feedback from its mobile customers.

Consider the following examples:

- Customers can send text messages as feedback about a delivery they received or take a survey about customer service.

- Listeners can send song requests or talking points to a DJ at a music station.

- Listeners can offer feedback to a talk show host.

Working with 160 Characters

Undoubtedly, you will find that your text message company is helpful in implementing your campaign, but you need to think about how to work a marketing message into 160 characters (not words, characters). This is the universal limit for text messages. In this case, you must make every letter and punctuation mark count. While you want to keep abbreviations brief for most people, you also want to maximize your communications in each message of only 160 characters. The younger the audience, the more abbreviations you can use. If you are texting to those who are new users or who are likely to be 30-plus years old, keep abbreviations to a minimum.

It is also critical to have a strong, clear call-to-action. In your strategic planning, start with the call-to-action. What do you want people to do after they receive your text message? Is it time to come into your store and use this text message as a coupon? Are customers texting you for more information, or have they agreed to a subscription? Do you want them to click through to your mobile website? The following text message is a sample I received after texting for more information about an industry trade show. Notice that the actions were in all caps so it was obvious what actions to take:

Mobile Mktg and Ent Expo Aug 27-28 2008 Javits Convention Ctr NY, NY Reply RATES for Booth Info MORE for info or CALL for Callback. Craig Henderson 555.123.5678

The following is an example of a text message coupon:

Show this msg to get 10 cent wings on any Tuesday at Wings R Us. 1234 Main St Anytown. Phone123.456.7890 Coupon Code 5678 Exp 12/31/08 Reply STOP to end.

Notice the address and phone number are included along with a coupon code that the restaurant staff can use to track redemption. In this case, customers can use the coupon on any Tuesday and for multiple uses. But you can give a one-time-use coupon as well. Remind your customers that they have already opted in to your campaign before they received this offer.

Movie Theater Advertising

Advertising in movie theaters can work better using mobile marketing as a direct response tool. Think about this: People grab their cell phones while those pre-movie public service announcements are shown (reminding people to turn off their phones), and when the movie ends, the first thing they do is turn their phones on again. Since they are already engaged with their phones while the movie ads are playing, give them a reason to respond to your ad. How about offering a coupon for dinner, dessert, or coffee after the movie, or a game at the bowling alley, or try engaging them in a trivia contest on their phone, or asking them to take a poll while they are waiting for the movie to begin. A delayed text message coupon can be sent to their phones while the movie is playing (and their phones are off). When they turn on their phones after the show, your coupon appears. Without this text message as a reminder, the customers can forget about your pre-movie offer. With it, you have the perfect offer that arrives at the right time while your audience is in the right place. You have created smart mobile marketing.

Choosing a Text Message Company

If you search for mobile marketing or text messaging, you will find dozens of companies to help you. In the Resources section at the end of this chapter, I recommend a few companies that I have experience with, but the ultimate choice will be yours. In choosing, you will decide based on the following five criteria: price, services offered, interface, carrier connectivity, and customer service.

Price

While a range of pricing strategies is available, the most common is offering a monthly fee for the software to implement your campaigns and a fee per message. This basic fee will usually include access to at least one keyword. You will often also see a set-up fee, additional keyword availability, and the associated price for messages exceeding your allocated amount. The range of prices can be outrageous when you see how much less expensively you can find the same services. There is a big difference in pricing for full-service campaigns (the vendor actually does the campaign for you) as opposed to self-service (where you do-it-yourself). Be sure you are comparing apples to apples when you are considering price.

Watch price and how the company is sending messages. A true SMS campaign has fees for each message even if it charges a flat price per number of messages. A texting campaign by email to the phones through the SMTP gateway will not. Being able to send free messages is one warning sign that you might be dealing with this type of technology. You should avoid an SMTP campaign for commercial text messaging.

Services Offered

All text message companies do not offer the same services. Some have voting, and some do not. Some offer contests, and some do not. Make sure your vendor can manage the types of campaigns you want to do. Some companies offer more than text messaging and can integrate other marketing services, such as email, voice direct mail, and faxing. If you need additional services, then be sure you are working with a company that offers what you need. Likewise, don't pay for any services you don't need. Often the companies that integrate other services cost more because they are doing more for you.

Interface

Ask to see a demo or sign up for a free trial to see how the program actually works. Some software will be easier to use than others. Find the one that will be the easiest for you. Best bet is to think about your campaign before you try out software or watch demos. Know what you want to accomplish and find the software to do what you want. You want to enhance your campaign with the right software. There are many types of text message software available that are easy to use.

Carrier Connectivity

Remember that not all text message companies work with all mobile phone carriers. If you know which carrier the majority of your customers use, then be sure to work with a company that connects to that carrier or find one that covers most. More companies will eventually work with all carriers, but be sure to find a vendor that works with as many carriers as possible to ensure your campaign's effectiveness right out of the gate.

Customer Service

Any decision you make about which company to work with involves customer service. Remember the sales team's customer service can be entirely different than the technical support team. Whenever possible, sign up for a free trial and use customer service to find out what help you will be getting if you need it. Take into account whether you will be getting help with your campaign. It costs more, but the expertise will likely save money in the long run.

Chapter Updates and Online Resource Guide

Updates to this chapter and its related Online Resource Guide are available at www.mobilemarketinghandbook.com/Updates/Texting.

The Online Resource Guide for Chapter 8 includes links for all sites listed in this chapter, as well as detailed reviews and current pricing information on text message companies.

Resources

The following resources are included to help you with further research and/or implementation of the ideas found in this chapter.

Text Message Companies

Blast Companies, www.blastcompanies.com
Club Texting, www.clubtexting.com
i2SMS, www.i2sms.com
mobileStorm, www.mobilestorm.com/freetrial/mmprofits
Mobivity, profits.mobilemarketing.net
TextMe for Business, www.textmeforbusiness.com

Creating a Mobile Web Presence

When asked whether they expect sites they visit frequently to provide a dedicated mobile version, a resounding 84 percent responded in the affirmative.

—From a study by iCrossing

What Is the Mobile Web?

The mobile web can be defined as the Internet accessed via a mobile device. However, that would be misleading because not everything on the Internet is built for use on mobile devices. The image of a small garden snake trying to swallow a basketball comes to mind. A smarter definition of the mobile web is a collection of mobile-friendly Internet sites that are accessible via mobile devices. Along with mobile websites, the mobile web includes mobile search engines, mobile advertising, and pay-per-click ads that are only displayed on mobile devices. The mobile web is a complete and distinct ecosystem for mobile devices.

When to Use the Mobile Web as a Marketing Tool

Unless your target market consists of people who never use mobile phones (which is unlikely if you are reading this book), your best bet is to create at least a simple mobile web presence as quickly as possible. We have reached a point in the marketing cycle of the Internet at which consumers expect businesses to have a website, even if it is a basic one. We will reach that point with the mobile web quickly as well. Your business needs to have a mobile website when consumers begin to expect a mobile web presence.

Think of this time as the gold rush of the mobile Internet. Now is the time to stake your claim. It is much the same as going back in time to 1995 and creating a website before all your competitors did. You can be among the first to have a mobile site and be available on the mobile web when your customers are looking for you out there.

Your mobile site can be as simple or as complex as your customers will need and use. Start out with a basic site. As consumer use of the mobile web increases from occasional by a few people to daily by most people, you can continue to add onto your mobile site. Start with what your customers or potential customers want to find (not search for, but find) as it relates to your business. Then, gradually add more features as your customers' needs change and your mobile marketing strategy develops.

How to Use the Mobile Web: Best Practices, Tips, and Techniques

Like the computer-based Internet, mobile involves two basic steps in creating a web presence: building a mobile website and driving traffic to it. Of course, there is also conversion—getting your customers to take the specific action you want them to take once they are on your site. For example, take a look at the formula for success on the mobile web in Figure 9.1.

Figure 9.1 The recipe for success on the mobile web is summed up in this box.

Content and Design

Setting aside all the technical aspects, which we will cover later in this chapter, the process of creating and designing content for a mobile site is different than it is for a full-size computer-accessible site. First of all, monitor size makes an obvious difference that changes everything. People do not "surf" on their phones. They don't browse; they look for exactly what they need in as few clicks as possible. They do not want irrelevant information or items that are impossible to deal with in a mobile environment. A site that is huge (from a bytes perspective) can easily cause a mobile phone to freeze or lock up, rendering it useless at precisely the moment when the user needs it the most. Consumers also don't want to find a diluted version of a site that is basically useless due to lack of content. The idea is to give your customers as much content as they want as quickly as possible.

What users need from you via a mobile website is also different because the information is totally dependent upon where they are, which is the entire concept of mobile. Keep in mind why someone is visiting your mobile site and then design it accordingly. Make it easy for them to find exactly what they need in as few clicks as possible (one click would be ideal). Peter Cranstone of 5o9, Inc., has a succinct way to think about design on the mobile web, which he originally learned from Ericsson, the world-renowned telecommunications company. He says: "Remember it's all about the 0-1-2-3 rule: 0 behavioral changes, 1 login point, 2 second download, 3 clicks to relevant content." Make sure that your customers don't have to change their behavior to use the services available on your mobile site. (Let them access the site via the browser they already use.) Provide visitors with a single action item that gets them going. Nothing should take longer than two seconds to download; within three clicks, they should have found what they are looking for on the site. If you follow this concept when strategizing your mobile website, you are laying a solid foundation for a usable, effective site.

Content Ideas for Your Mobile Website

The strategy of effective mobile web content should not be taken lightly. Put yourself in your customers' shoes and give them what they are looking for as quickly as possible. Think about where they are likely to be viewing your site: on a bus or subway, sitting in their cars at a stop light, standing on a street corner, or sitting at a restaurant. Not surprisingly, another study by iCrossing ("How America Searches Using Mobile") found that maps and directions are the top items that people seek using mobile search. Additionally, your customers will want other specific things from you on your mobile website, and they may want more and more over time. To get started, here are some ideas about what to include on your mobile website. Of course, you will have other things that make sense for your particular business or industry, as well:

- Maps/directions to your business

- Business hours

- Click-to-call button

- List of items/brands you carry (your menu)

- Fresh content in small chunks

- Timely information about your business

- Special offers

- Event information

What you don't put on your mobile website can be as important as what you do. For example, don't include:

- Excess graphics (size or quantity)

- Long articles

- Anything that takes more than three clicks to find

- Large files/downloads that could cause a mobile device to crash or freeze

Determining Site Flow and Click Depth

With mobile sites, it is extremely important to ensure a smooth flow for site visitors. It should be easy to navigate the site and find what is there. It also should be obvious and easy to get back to the home page from anywhere in the site. In fact, index cards are the perfect tool for sketching out your mobile site because they are the ideal size to remind you how much information you can squeeze onto a mobile website. You can also move them around easily to determine the flow of a website. Start by turning them vertically to simulate a small vertical screen. Then write on the index card what you want to include on each page. It if doesn't fit easily on the index card, then it won't fit on your customers' mobile screen. Laying out the index cards side by side can also give you a snapshot of exactly how many clicks it will take someone to reach the deepest level of content, which is the click depth. Three clicks is the maximum number of clicks that I recommend on a mobile website. More than that and you will frustrate your visitors.

Conversion: Getting Your Customers to Do What You Want Them to Do

The art of getting people to do what you want them to on your website (mobile or desktop) is called conversion. Your ability to convert people successfully from a site visitor to a customer, a caller, or an opted-in person on your SMS or email list is the key to your success on the web. After all, if you have millions of people who visit your site, but they don't engage with you further, then your site will not be successful. You may think that this is not the case if you simply sell advertising based on your traffic. However, if your advertisers don't get the exposure they want, then you won't get return advertisers, and your site will fail. Even if you are a retail store and offer your location, hours, and other information for your customers, there is still conversion involved—getting these mobile web visitors to physically visit your place of business. Make sure you get people to take action while they are on your site.

The best way to get people to take action is tell them what to do, and then make it easy for them to do it. Google is an excellent example. A person who wants to search on a topic is given one thing to do on the Google home page: input what he is looking for and hit the search button. Google has nearly a 100 percent conversion rate. People who go to the Google home page do what Google wants them to do. You won't be able to get your conversion rate that high, but you certainly want it as high as possible. Make sure your call-to-action is prominent on your mobile site. If you want people to sign up for an SMS, put your short code and keyword call-to-action on the site. If you are building an email list, put your email sign-up box where it is clearly visible. If you are selling on your mobile site, make the order process obvious. Ideally, you should link to the call-to-action information from every page on the site.

Giving people the option to sample your wares creates a great conversion strategy. Show people a sample of your newsletter, send them an introductory text message, or if you are selling something, give them a free trial offer before buying. UpSNAP.com, the leading site in mobile audio, reported a 25 percent conversion rate when using free trial offers for paid subscriptions.

Another component in a successful conversion is giving people a reason to do what you want them to do. If you want people to opt in to a text message campaign from your mobile website, tell them why they should. What value will they receive from it? Even if something is free, spell out what people will receive. If it is compelling enough, they will do it, and your conversion rate increases. If you don't provide enough value for your visitors, they will not do what you ask, and your conversion will decrease. It may seem simple enough on paper, but the tracking and analysis of actual site visitors will provide more details to help you discover all the complexities. Tracking your site visitors is covered in depth in Chapter 6.

Building a Mobile Website

In many ways, creating a mobile site might seem easier than building a full-service site. First of all, mobile sites are smaller and contain much less information than a wired Internet site. Building a website has become so easy for so many people that it would seem that building a mobile website would be at least as simple. But it is not as straightforward as it seems, since more than 5,000 different models of mobile devices are available for consumers, and dozens of different mobile browsers load on a multitude of different operating systems. To top it off, a different cell phone carrier serves each of these variations. Technologically, it is almost impossible for any site to be displayed correctly on all mobile devices. The mobile web has a long way to go before it is as effortless as the Internet for consumers to use. Still, there are ways to maximize the number of people who can accurately access your mobile site. It may be done for you by transcoding services, or you can build your mobile site using one of four specific strategies: one web, miniaturizing, mobilizing, and personalizing.

Transcoding

As a way of helping consumers experience the mobile web with few errors when they access a full-size website on their mobile devices, companies such as Novarra offer a service called transcoding. Transcoding essentially strips a website to its basics and integrates the essential items in a mobile-friendly format whenever it is accessed via a mobile phone. So a person accessing a website built for computer access on their mobile devices would automatically have the site turned into a mobile-accessible site. While this may sound like the perfect solution to the technological nightmare of mobile site delivery, it is actually quite controversial. When Vodafone UK first launched its transcoding service in Europe in 2007, it made transcoding an automatic function for all websites being accessed by mobile devices. As a result, many mobile-specific websites were also stripped of all graphics and presented to the end user. The sites were already mobile friendly and having them transcoded was actually taking away functionality of the sites and wasting the efforts of the businesses that created mobile specific sites. It is highly frustrating for businesses to have built a mobile site and not have it presented to customers.

Fortunately, Novarra started transcoding only those sites not already mobile friendly. The way to indicate that your site is created especially for mobile is to include some specific code in your site. See the Online Resource Guide for links to the most up-to-date information on transcoding and what code to include on your mobile site.

Mobile Site Strategy

As you start building your mobile site, your attention will likely be on the technology involved in actually constructing the site. While technology is important, your single most important focus must be what your customers want and need. The content of your mobile site will ultimately be more important than whatever technology you use to build the site. Make sure you don't lose sight of the customer. The sections that follow provide more information about the four schools of thought about mobile web strategy (one web, miniaturizing, mobilizing, and personalizing) and how each strategy impacts your customers.

One Web

One prominent school of thought about mobile web strategy quickly loses sight of the customer: the idea that "one web" exists and that people want the "same experience on their mobile devices as they want on their computers." Despite what Apple iPhone commercials and proponents of this strategy lead us to believe, this is not the case. Here's why: Sitting at my desk, I have a 17-inch monitor, a full keyboard, and enough computing power to handle whatever the Internet offers. But my mobile device has about a 2-inch monitor tapping into minimal computing power, and I use my thumbs to type on the QWERTY keyboard. (Some mobile users don't even have that luxury and are triple tapping on their number pads to spell out words.) I also use my mobile device somewhere other than the comfort of my quiet home or office. Why would I want the same thing delivered to me regardless of which device I use? Why would anyone? People do not want the same experience on their mobile web that they do on a desktop computer, despite what many people in the mobile industry may tell you.

As my colleague Giff Gfroerer from i2SMS says, "The mobile web is about: quick finds not searching; quick information not browsing; quick views not watching; quick payments not shopping. It is making your customer's life easier by solving a problem!" He's right. People on the mobile web are using it completely differently than they use the Internet on full-size computers. Yet many in the industry continue to teach that there is one web experience.

This argument stems from the fact that millions of people worldwide only access the Internet through their mobile devices. They don't have a desktop computer with Internet access. Of course, those people want to have the same experience on mobile as on their desktops because they have no other access point. However, this book is primarily written for a North American audience, and roughly 70 percent of the population in the U.S.

and in Canada has access to the Internet via desktop computer. This is a big difference from the worldwide Internet penetration of 19 percent. Unless you are specifically targeting a global audience, your customers can choose which of your sites they want to access using whatever device they choose, whether a full-size computer or a mobile device. It is true that some North American mobile users in lower-income urban centers and in some ethnic populations have web and mobile user patterns that closely match those of the rest of the world without easy access to the Internet, but that still doesn't mean they want to cram the full Internet into their phones.

When the Apple iPhone was launched, its commercials showed the amazing device accessing various websites that looked the same as they do on a full-size monitor. This played heavily into the concept of people wanting the same experience on the mobile web as on the computer-accessed web. But even with the overwhelming response the iPhone received and the increasing numbers of units in the marketplace, use of this mobile device still represents just a fraction of the number of phones in consumers' hands. Even with the projected 10 million unit sales by the end of 2008, this represents only 4 percent of the total subscribers in the U.S. And the iPhone only became available in Canada in mid-2008. So while the users of this one device may have the closest experience of the desktop web on mobile, it is not viable for a business to build its entire strategy around 4 percent of its users, no matter how enticing those commercials are.

While it would be easier for businesses and consumers alike if websites and the experience of using them were magically the same, it is physically and technologically impossible. People use the Internet differently based on where they are and what device (even an iPhone) they are using to access the web.

Miniaturizing Your Website

Another option for dealing with the mobile web is to build a single site, promote a single URL, and then use technology to determine how users will be viewing it. If they are on a computer, it will deliver the computer-size version. If the user is viewing on a mobile device, the site will display in a mobile-size version by dynamically generating the content in a smaller size without graphics. In this strategy, the content is essentially the same, only the size of what is displayed changes. This is the technology that GetMobile.com Juicer service and FeedM8 use. Essentially, any site is accessible to mobile devices through these services. The new miniature sites will work error free on mobile devices, but the content remains the same.

Building a Mobile Website
Specifically for iPhones

Even though they are only 4 percent of the total market of cell phone users in the U.S. (and will likely have a similar market share in Canada), iPhone users are the most voracious users of the mobile web. A January 2008 report released by M:Metrics showed that while only 13.1 percent of all U.S. cell phone users accessed news or other information via a mobile browser, an astounding 84.8 percent of iPhone users had. Smartphone users weighed in at 58.2 percent. Given that statistic, it may be worthwhile to create an iPhone-specific website.

While any mobile website you build will certainly work on iPhones, it won't take advantage of the special functions of the iPhone, such as using your fingers to pinch or slide to enlarge or reduce a site. In addition to creating a generic mobile-friendly site, you can create a specific version for iPhone users. Special coding needs to be built into your website to allow your site visitors to use all the functions of an iPhone. If you want to add iPhone-specific features on your mobile site, the best place for your web designer to begin is at the Apple iPhone Dev Center (developer.apple.com/iphone).

While error free is certainly better than a site that won't even load, it is not the same as focusing on what your customers want. This miniature website strategy isn't a long-term solution. You can make the same content accessible via the phone, but the reality is that your users need different information and faster access, not just the same text without the graphics. Clearly, mobile web users are not searching for a multiple-page document that would require the patience of a saint to scroll through on their tiny mobile screens. Most likely, they are looking for a specific subset of the information that is available on a complete computer-based site. So you could start by miniaturizing your site as quickly as possible so it is at least visible on mobile when your customers look for you. But don't stop there; you have more work to do. For example, take a look at what my site looks like on a desktop (Figure 9.2) compared to what it looks like in a miniaturized version (Figure 9.3).

Figure 9.2   Here is my website MobileMarketingProfits.com as it appears on my desktop monitor.

Figure 9.3   Here is my website miniaturized using FeedM8. Notice that the ads are unrelated to the subject matter that appears. The long articles on my site are not content a person would want to read on a tiny screen. Yes, my site is readable on mobile, but it is not the best option.

Mobilizing Your Website

You also have the option of building two completely different sites: one for desktop computers and one for mobile devices. Then, you can market two different URLs, and let the users decide which site to visit based on how what device they are using and what they are doing, whether browsing (on their desktops) or finding (via their mobile devices).

The popular cooking site AllRecipes.com already adopted this strategy. Users who visit www.allrecipes.com via a desktop computer see a robust site with photos, recipes, ads, contests, mini articles, and even a Cook of the Week feature (Figure 9.4). The content is perfect for viewing on a desktop-size computer (something I might do on a Saturday morning with a cup of coffee and my grocery list by my side).

When I grab my trusty Treo and log on to m.allrecipes.com (something I might do while standing in the grocery store aisle trying to figure out what to make for dinner tonight), I can instantly access an easy-to-use search box and an ingredient search link. To find a recipe, all I have to do is enter one search term and press the submit button. The mobile site is designed for mobile use (Figure 9.5).

But if I accidentally forget to type in the "m" of the domain name while using my mobile device, I see the computer-size allrecipes.com site on my mobile device (Figure 9.6), which is not easy to use if I am standing in the grocery store aisle. I have to scroll around to see what I want. It is similar to looking at the big site but through a tiny window instead. It is a totally different experience and not a pleasant one at that. To help alleviate this situation, you should have a link to your mobile site at the top left of your computer-based site. The reason for this is two-fold: Not only will people who have stumbled upon the desktop site on their mobile device be able to quickly get to the right size and right content site for mobile, but it will also promote your mobile site to folks who are browsing via their desktop computers.

Try using this mobile-specific site strategy in addition to your main website. This is what your customers want from you. Remember, 84 percent of people want a site specifically dedicated to mobile use, according to the iCrossing study noted at the beginning of this chapter. You can market them as distinct sites; you can distribute your sitename.com URL and your mobile site URL. While this may seem to be double-duty in the marketing department, it is helpful in making people aware that you have a mobile site available. Until the time that accessing the web with a mobile device is as common as going online from a full-size computer, you will need to educate and remind your customers about the mobile site option.

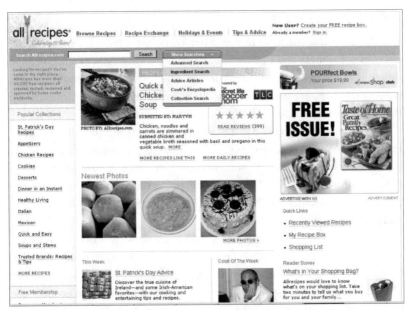

Figure 9.4   This is www.allrecipes.com as seen on a desktop monitor. Notice how many different articles and options are displayed.

Figure 9.5   This is the AllRecipes mobile site accessed on my mobile using www.m.allrecipes.com. Notice how the site is designed specifically for mobile and how easy it would be to use the site in a mobile environment.

Figure 9.6   *This is the AllRecipes site accessed on my mobile using*
www.allrecipes.com (I did not insert the m in the URL), with the
desktop-size site being delivered on my mobile. Notice that this
site is not easy to access or use in a mobile environment.

Having a distinct URL for your mobile site will help you in distributing this
marketing message.

Personalizing Your Website

Ideally, you want to create two or more groups of content (one for desktop
and at least one for mobile) yet only have one website address (your
sitename.com) to market. Customers can go online either on their desktops
(Figure 9.7) or mobile devices (Figure 9.8), type in one URL, and go to the
right site. When a visitor accesses your site, the site automatically detects
which set of content to display based on which type of device (computer or
mobile) the visitor is using. This approach, which major sites including
CNN.com and Google already use, requires a bit more technology behind
the scenes, but it's worth it. This is the future of accessibility via the mobile
web. Even though the end user will have one website address to use, this
strategy is different than the "one web" philosophy because there are two
different sets of content being presented to that consumer.

Making this mobile web solution a reality can be a bit complex, so I'll
keep the tech-speak to a minimum. One option is to program your site to
recognize the user agent field, a small bit of information that is sent to a
website server when it is accessed that tells the server what kind of computer is visiting. The server then delivers either computer or mobile content

Figure 9.7   The CNN.com site on a desktop is quite robust with plenty of features and stories displayed above the fold for viewers to see.

Figure 9.8   This is the CNN Mobile site delivered on my mobile. I entered the same URL as I did from my desktop computer, and the CNN site understood that I was looking at it from a mobile browser, hence sending the mobile version.

to your users, based on what device they are using. Websites that "grab" user agent data can determine whether the user is accessing the website via an iPhone, Windows Mobile, BlackBerry, or carrier-supplied browser. This lets the site deliver specific mobile content that takes advantage of iPhone features or is specifically sized to a standard Verizon-type screen. The user agent is accurate at least 90 percent of the time. The limitation is that the site is dependent on the browser, not the device. For example, AT&T Tilt users can access a website with their MediaNet browsers, and the website might "think" it is a RAZR or other feature phone. The same device, using the Windows Mobile browser, has twice the screen dimensions. Although a site can detect the content is for a mobile user, it still leaves some things to chance. This approach lets a site deliver full-screen or mobile-screen content best built to the least common denominator.

Some of the mobile website builders, including MoFuse, offer codes you can use on your site to create this automatic redirect feature. You can also find other sources for user agent codes in the Resources section at the end of this chapter. Even though it is not yet foolproof, it is still usable.

You can also allow visitors to customize their mobile experience by setting up parameters and settings on their desktop computers. When they visit your mobile site, they can sign in using a customized URL and use the settings they created. But there is a downside: You will have to build a database for all these customer preferences and manage the technology to run it.

Another option is to use personalization software, from companies such as 5o9, Inc. This software plugs into a web server and a customer's mobile browser (no new hardware or applications to learn) and tells any website the precise real-time capabilities of the device that is accessing that website. In addition to serving the best version of the website for the device, it can offer so much more. Wouldn't it be helpful to automatically warn your customers, "Your battery is at 4 percent; are you sure you want to download this information or video?" or give them the option to access GPS data or keep personal information (such as name, address, or log-in information) encrypted on their phones to reduce the data entry required on a tiny keyboard? This makes it easier for your customers to order a pizza, get directions to your store, or access your services from their mobile devices. This is an important point: Your customers control their personal information. You can deliver a personalized experience without building online profiles and storing personal identifying data.

While this technology currently supports only smartphones (BlackJacks, BlackBerrys, Treos, and others), it reflects how quickly mobile technology is adjusting to the needs of mobile users and making big-company capabilities affordable to small and mid-sized businesses. If you are outsourcing your development or hosting, ask your service provider to investigate these options.

Mobile Site Creation Options

Once you have determined the content for your mobile site and which web strategy you are going to use (one web, miniaturizing, mobilizing, or personalizing), you are ready to build your mobile site. Of course, if you are working with an agency, it will take care of it for you. If you're building your own mobile site or seeking the right vendor, following are your options.

Miniaturizing Mobile Sites

To get your current site miniaturized so it will show up on mobile devices error free, you can use a variety of free or low-cost services. You will have to submit your main site URL to a miniaturizing service, and then a mobile version of your site will be created from your existing content. It is likely that graphics will be stripped out or reduced in size. If you have a blog, it will be easy to mobilize your site. If you have a site that does not have an RSS feed, you may find you spend more time miniaturizing your big site than you would just building a mobile one from scratch. See the Resources at the end of this chapter for a list of mobile sites that specialize in miniaturization.

Mobile Platform Providers

Companies such as iLoopMobile, GoLive! Mobile, and Crisp Wireless offer complete A-to-Z solutions for mobile site building, advertising, text messaging, and marketing, along with reporting. If you have the budget to work with such companies, this is the way to go. You'll have content management at your fingertips, easy software to work with, and all the tools your heart could desire. You'll probably wonder what all the fuss is about with the mobile web. It'll be like driving on the freeway in the high occupancy lane as you are whizzing by a huge traffic jam. Check the Resources section at the end of this chapter for a list of mobile platform providers. The Online Resource Guide also has reviews of their services with current pricing ranges.

Mobile Website Designers

Another more complicated option is custom building a mobile website and hosting it. Unless you are a web designer or have an in-house design team who is familiar with mobile, you will need to hire a person or firm to do this. If you currently work with designers, you may be able to work with them on your mobile site design. But not many web designers have worked with mobile yet and may not be prepared for what awaits them. If you want to work with someone in particular, share this book with them, and go over the site strategy you are planning to implement. Then, point them to two important resources that will help along the way. The first is dev.mobi, which is a site for web designers who want to learn about mobile design.

The information on the site will keep your designer on the right track while providing tools and information. Second, *Mobile Web Design* by Cameron Moll (www.mobilewebbook.com) is a book with helpful information. Both should help your web design team get ready to design for mobile. Do not proceed with a design firm that says it can design a mobile site without any proof of its track record or without the firm agreeing to get help from these resources. Check the Resources section at the end of this chapter for a list of mobile web designers.

Mobile Site Builders

If you are committed to building a mobile website but don't like any of the previously mentioned options because of budgetary constraints or other reasons, you can use a mobile site builder. The good news is that you can use one of several free or low-cost site builders. The down side is that you will likely invest a decent amount of sweat equity in getting it done. And your site may not be as fully functional or as pleasant to look at as sites done on a mobile platform or built by a designer. But at least you'll be on mobile with a site that's built specifically for mobile use, and you won't spend a fortune. You can test out what works, find out what your customers want more of, and get your customers to try mobile marketing. When the pricing drops on the other options, you can always upgrade to those solutions. See the Resources section at the end of this chapter for mobile site builders.

What Domain Name to Use

If you choose to go with a game plan of using two distinct websites (one for desktop browsing and one for mobile finding), you will need a mobile site URL. At this point, there is no clear standard for how to name your mobile site. The options in use are: sitename.mobi, m.sitename.com, mobile.site name.com, or sitename.com/mobile. My recommendation is to go with sitename.mobi. It is likely that the .mobi extension will become the most commonly used and is instantly recognizable as a mobile URL. Additionally, using a .mobi domain is a solid mobile SEO strategy (more about this in Chapter 10).

Mobile Site Hosting

You can host your mobile site at the same host that you use for your computer site. There is no need to get mobile specific hosting. Technically speaking, there is only one web. The only thing you might want to do is to find a web host that understands mobile and already offers mobile services enabled by technologies such as 5o9 Content Manager software, mobile coupon generation, and texting or email marketing services. This would make your mobile web building experience go that much more smoothly. Check the Online Resource Guide for web hosts that offer mobile personalization software.

Driving Traffic to Your Mobile Website

Just as with any website, driving traffic to it is crucial to the success of the site. You cannot build a mobile site and just wait for people to discover it. Even now, in the early days of the mobile web gold rush, it is not possible. You must proactively work to drive visitors to your mobile site; plan on continuing this part of your mobile web presence campaign indefinitely.

Marketing Integration

As I have noted throughout the book, the best way to drive traffic to your mobile campaign is by weaving your mobile call-to-action into your existing marketing. This is especially true of driving website traffic. Mobile marketing is all about interaction with existing marketing (see Chapter 5).

Mobile Web Promotion Strategies

In addition to driving visitors through your existing marketing, you can use mobile search, mobile advertising (including mobile pay-per-click), and mobile publicity tactics, which are all covered in Chapter 10.

Chapter Updates and Online Resource Guide

Updates to this chapter and its related Online Resource Guide are available at www.MobileMarketingHandbook.com/Updates/MobileWeb.

The Online Resource Guide for Chapter 9 includes links for all sites listed in this chapter, as well as:

- A comprehensive list and detailed reviews of mobile web-building solutions, including platforms, miniaturizers, designers, and builders

- Links to examples of mobile websites, reviews of mobile sites, and some of the marketing from companies to promote their sites

- Updated information about transcoding

Resources

The following resources are included to help you with further research and/or implementation of the ideas found in this chapter.

User Agent Codes

Mobile Web Developer: MobileRedirect, www.mobilewebdeveloper.com

Miniaturizers

FeedM8, www.feedm8.com
GetMobile Juicer, www.getmobile.com
MoFuse, www.mofuse.com
Winksite, www.winksite.com

Mobile Platform Providers

Crisp Wireless, www.crispwireless.com
GoLive! Mobile, www.golivemobile.com
iLoop Mobile, www.iloopmobile.com

Mobile Site Builders

MoFuse, www.mofuse.com
Winksite, www.winksite.com

Mobile Web Designers

Fling Media, www.flingmedia.com
Little Springs Design, www.littlespringsdesign.com

Certified Web Developers

dev.mobi: Certified DotMobi Web Developers,
    dev.mobi/content/certified-dotmobi-web-developers

Resources for Mobile Web Designers

5o9, Inc., www.5o9inc.com
Apple iPhone Development Fling Media, www.flingmedia.com
dev.mobi, www.dev.mobi
Mobile Design, log.mobiledesign.org

Articles

Craig Hockenberry, "Put Your Content in My Pocket," A List Apart, www.alistapart.com/articles/putyourcontentinmypocket

Books

Ajit Jaokar and Tony Fish, *Mobile Web 2.0* (futuretext, 2006)
Cameron Moll, *Mobile Web Design* (Lulu.com, 2008), www.mobileweb book.com

Mobile Web Promotion Strategies

Mobile SEO reshapes the boundaries of social media vs science. The core premise of discovery on mobile is reflected in how difficult it is to manipulate a new pure mobile medium—for the business and the consumer.

—Bena Roberts, MobileSEONews.com

Within the framework of the mobile web, powerful promotion strategies can be used to drive traffic to your mobile website, create brand awareness, and augment your publicity campaign. You're likely to be familiar with these tools because there are similar tools on the Internet. You may think you already know about them because of their similarity to those on the Internet, but don't be fooled. There is everything from nuances to huge differences when you're dealing with mobile.

What Is Mobile Search?

I remember the first time I found out about Google. When I complained that I couldn't find some research online to my friend Mary, who was steps ahead of me on the technology path, she asked if I had tried Google yet. After my first Google search, I was hooked. Obviously I am not the only person who feels this way. The day will come when we won't be able to imagine life without our favorite mobile search tool (which may or may not be Google Mobile) either. In business, you now have to work to get your mobile sites listed in mobile search engines so that customers can find you when they search for you specifically or for what you offer generically.

Essentially, mobile search is the search engine for the mobile web. It includes the built-in search tools found on phones that carriers provide, and it is more well-known through search engines such as Google, Yahoo!, and MSN that serve mobile-friendly results from a mobile-friendly search interface.

When to Use Mobile Search as a Marketing Tool

As soon as you have established your mobile website online, begin your mobile search marketing campaign. If you plan on waiting to tackle your mobile search strategy, don't. In the early days of Internet search, the new search engines were practically begging for sites to list for their visitors. The same is true now in mobile search and in mobile advertising. The law of supply and demand is in your favor, but it won't be for long.

How to Use Mobile Search: Best Practices, Tips, and Techniques

The basic concept of search engine optimization (SEO) is to get your site to show up when someone searches for it. SEO strategies are used on the Internet and on the mobile web. Consumers can search for specific data (they search for your company) or for general information (they search for a broad term). Search engines show your site because 1) they know your site exists, and 2) something on your site matches with what the searcher was seeking. SEO is actually how you let search engines know your site exists and that your site contains the right information for the right searches. Since the topic of search engine optimization is worth an entire book of its own, I will cover what you need to know about mobile search; if you need additional or background knowledge on overall search engine marketing, see the Resources section at the end of the chapter.

How Is Mobile Search Different than Desktop Search?

You know that being listed in desktop search engines is critical to your website's success. This is also true of your mobile site. Mobile search is different, though: Users search using different search engines, they search in different ways, and the results that are displayed are handled differently.

The mobile search environment is different than computer-based search because there are two pathways for consumers to search. One is on-portal/on-deck (the default search engines set up by the mobile carriers), and the other is off-portal (search engines such as Google and Yahoo! that are not affiliated with a mobile carrier). On-portal search only shows the results listed within the carrier's on-portal directory (a list of sites the carriers have compiled). No other sites are shown. This is often referred to as the "walled garden." Essentially, this means that your cell phone carrier is actually the search engine. For consumers with a basic phone or for consumers who are not especially tech-savvy, it is likely they will use the on-deck search engine exclusively in the near future. It is just easier to use what is already there with one click than it is to figure out how to access the open mobile web. On-portal searchers will find fewer sites, but every site will be mobile friendly.

Most phones and cell phone carriers provide an on-portal search engine but still allow access to search engines such as Google and Yahoo! or whatever search venue a customer chooses. In off-portal search, the user starts with the mobile web first and then searches on Google Mobile or Yahoo! oneSearch. In this case, the user can find any site listed in these search engines. This is what the computer web search experience is like and what consumers already know. Off-portal searching is still a bit wild; it is likely that a consumer will be directed to a site that a mobile device cannot easily access. There will be more sites to choose from, but the results may be disappointing until the search engines' inventory of mobile sites meets mobile-searcher demand.

One major difference between mobile and desktop search is how the results are displayed. Results are often displayed based on the device being used. For example, a person using a Motorola RAZR for mobile search might obtain entirely different results than someone searching with a Nokia N95. This is different than desktop search because desktop results are consistent from user to user. A person searching on a Dell with an Acer monitor sees the same results as someone using an HP computer with an HP monitor. Mobile search is clearly more complex than desktop search.

Lastly, fewer results are shown on a mobile search engine results page than on a desktop version. On desktop search, people rarely go beyond the first 10 results on the first page of search results. On a mobile search, only two, three, or four results are shown, and people are even less likely to go to a second page of search results. This makes it more important to take your mobile SEO strategies seriously while you can still be listed on the first page of search results for your keyword.

The bottom line is that mobile search is different than desktop Internet search for the consumer and the website builder. The tactics that work for SEO on the Internet do not necessarily work for mobile search. For example, incoming links do not yet make a big impact on whether your mobile site appears in search engines. Likewise, actions that simply make no difference for your search engine ranking on the desktop web, such as submitting your site to Google, Yahoo!, or other search engines, can make a huge impact for your mobile site.

Mobile SEO Tactics

SEO strategies for desktop websites are enough to fill books, weekend seminars, and multiweek online courses. Fortunately, mobile search engine strategies are less complicated, at least for now. So jump in while the process is still simple.

Create a Mobile-Friendly Website

To ensure that you have good optimization for your mobile site, develop a true mobile-friendly website as described in the "Mobilizing Your Website" and "Personalizing Your Website" sections of Chapter 9. This is important because mobile search engines are designed to deliver mobile sites. This is what their customers want and what keeps them in business. Error messages can also appear for sites that do not render well on mobile devices. Search engines don't like to deliver sites that produce error messages. This means that people doing a mobile search and coming across your desktop site on their mobile will limit your mobile SEO if they get an error when they click in. And the more sites that mobile users click into that are not easy to use on their mobile, the longer it will take for the mobile web to be widely used. If the search process is not easy, then people will stay away. Life is too short to waste time on sites that aren't easy to use, so make sure your main website will work on mobile (miniaturize it at least) so you don't completely obliterate your mobile search engine possibilities.

Be Visible to Local-Focused Searchers

Location-based search is more important in mobile searching than it is on the desktop; sites that are optimized for local search will fare better in mobile search engine results than sites that are not. After all, location-based information is the No. 1 type of data that people search for on the mobile web. People are looking for places and services around them, where they are now. It is your job to offer this content, and the search engines will reward you for it. This is local search in an entirely new light. If you have a business that caters to local users, even in multiple locations, consider your mobile web presence for locations. People must find you when they search for you and that includes your keyword and city name in an off-portal search. Likewise, make sure you are listed in places that feed local data on the on-portal search engines.

To ensure your site is optimized for local search, your city, state, and ZIP code should be easy to find on your site in several places. Use your city name and state in text (not a graphic) on your home page and your contact

How to Help Search Engines Find Your Mobile Site

This is a great tip from blogger Bryson Meunier (Natural Search and Mobile SEO Blog, www.brysonmeunier.com) about Mobile SEO. It ensures that your mobile website is delivered to mobile searchers and not your more highly ranked desktop site. This code will alert Google that if searchers are using their mobile search engine, your mobile site should be displayed even if your main site is actually what should be served to them based on Google rankings. To help Google find your mobile website, put this tag in your computer-based page:

```
<link rel="alternate" media="handheld"
xhref="http://mobile.website.com/">
```

Note: Substitute your mobile URL in the space where this code reads http://mobile.website.com/.

page, and include a map/directions page with text-based information and a link to a map.

On-portal search engines list your business on local-based sites such as Google Local, Yahoo! Local, AskCity, Live Search Maps, MojoPages, Citysearch, and others. This is the best way to guarantee good local search optimization. Check the Mobile Search Submission Action Plan in the Online Resource Guide for a complete, updated listing of all sites with local search listings.

Mobile users who may not want to access the mobile web or cannot get online (while driving) will also use voice search. This involves calling a phone number such as 1-800-GOOG-411 and searching verbally. This is not the high-tech tool it seems to be; this is just calling information, which is something consumers have been doing for years. But the big deal is that they are doing it while they are out in the world ready to take action instantly. To be listed in GOOG-411's voice search, just list your business in Google's free Local Business Center.

Mobile Search Engine Submission

Clearly you need to submit your mobile site so people can find it via on-portal and off-portal search engines. Before you start imagining the futility of contacting each individual cell phone carrier to get your mobile site listed on its built-in search engines, it is likely the cell phone carriers are using a white label solution from one of the top mobile search companies where you can submit your site. Yes, it is possible to submit your mobile site now to the major mobile search engines and get it listed just like in the good old days of the Internet. Mobile search engines (on- and off-portal) need more mobile sites to serve to their visitors. There are also several mobile site directories where you can submit your site because they are looking for mobile content to share. It is up to you to create your mobile-friendly site and then submit it.

Keyword Research

The crucial concept in any SEO campaign (desktop or mobile) is knowing what words your customers are using when they search. As with your desktop website, you need to do keyword research for your topic. But unlike with desktop search, there are not a variety of keyword research tools. They are simply not available yet because mobile search is so new. So for now, you have to do it the old-fashioned way by getting to know your customers. Figure out what they would type into their search box while using their mobile phones when they want to find you.

Short keyword phrases are going to be more common. After all, it is harder for mobile users to type in a long search phrase using their phone keypads. Use basic keywords for people to find you. Start by thinking of one-word keywords that would lead your customers to you. The following ideas will help you figure out what your customers might use for their searches:

- People often search for brand names. Include your own brand name and your URL in the keywords you want displayed in a search.

- Missing spaces are common. It is not easy to hit the space bar on a phone, so it is quite common for two words to become one. If you have some good two-word phrases, you should list both "two words" and "twowords" in your keyword list.

- The combination of location + keyword is popular. There is also a widely used combination of free + keyword.

- Cell-related searches (things people do or use on their cell phones) are common; people are literally thinking mobile when they are searching mobile.

- People often search for exact domains. Consumers can use the easily located search bar to launch their browsers. Instead of launching their browsers and then searching, they may be entering a URL into the search box, hitting submit, and launching their browsers. Put your URL on your keyword list.

Until the keyword research tools that automate keyword marketing become common, we are on our own. It will be survival of the smartest, not survival of the one with the best tools. Your intelligence and creativity will be on your side in the beginning of mobile keywords. Enjoy it while it lasts.

What Is Mobile Advertising?

Although mobile marketing is sometimes referred to as mobile advertising, in this section I am specifically discussing advertising that is on the mobile web. Consumers have already accepted this form of advertising because it is not as disruptive as a text message or a Bluetooth opt-in prompt. It simply shows up when they are on the mobile web. Consumers are used to seeing advertising on a website. Businesses are also comfortable with mobile advertising because it is most like the advertising and marketing they are already doing on the Internet.

Mobile advertising is comprised of graphic banners, sponsorships, and text-link ads that appear on mobile websites. Mobile advertising is growing exponentially, and industry analysts are predicting this growth to continue. For example, JackMyers Media Business Report projects that mobile advertising spending will increase to $2.44 billion in 2009, and eMarketer predicts U.S. mobile ads will grow to $4.75 billion in 2011.

When to Use Mobile Advertising as a Marketing Tool

Mobile ads can be used for branding, mobile site traffic generation, and a range of direct response campaigns. If you have a branding budget and your target audience is likely to fall into the power mobile user group, then mobile ads are an excellent tool to increase your brand awareness. If you have a mobile site and want to drive traffic to it, then you will find that mobile advertising is an excellent source of traffic. When you want a campaign that is ultimately trackable and makes it easy to prove your ROI (return on investment), then consider building your mobile advertising campaign as a direct response campaign.

Mobile advertising is one of the fastest mobile marketing tools to implement. The major ad networks have self-serve options. You simply create your campaign and launch it. If you want a campaign that you can launch quickly, mobile advertising can fit the bill.

How to Use Mobile Advertising: Best Practices, Tips, and Techniques

While it is true that the more relevant you can make your ad to your audience, the better your response will be, this strategy has never been easier to implement than with mobile advertising. Mobile ad networks can gather data about the person who is searching via mobile (and who will receive your ad), which is not possible with any other marketing medium. Ad networks can tell exactly what type of phone is being used to visit a particular website. The networks also know what search brought the user to that site. In some cases, they even have a search history and can link this search to previous ones to deliver relevant ads to the user based on the cumulative effect of their search.

Despite the privacy issues that are likely to ensue (see Chapter 3), this is good for the consumer and the advertiser alike. Compare a person reading a newspaper to someone reading a news article on her cell phone. First, in a 50-page newspaper with 25 percent advertising, the advertising includes dozens of ads. The remaining 75 percent of content is a collection of articles, sidebars, and other material. Neither the reader nor any of the advertisers assume that 100 percent of the advertising in the newspaper is relevant to any one particular reader. Actually, both sides don't see that 100 percent of the content is relevant either. When someone chooses to read a news article on a mobile site, advertising will also appear. This ad, which will likely take up 25 percent of the screen space, will be the only ad. In this case, the reader and the advertiser assume it will be relevant to the reader. After all, it is the only ad and the reader has given up 25 percent of reading space to an ad that will seem like part of the content if it is relevant and will seem annoying if it is not. Undoubtedly, relevance in mobile advertising is the most critical best practice to advertisers and consumers. It is through working with your ad network that you will be able to target your ad to people who will find it the most relevant.

Building Brand Awareness via Mobile Advertising

If you have a brand awareness campaign to implement and you want to use mobile, mobile advertising is the tool you need. It is excellent for branding, especially when you use graphic banner ads and sponsorships. Since ads can be delivered to select consumers, you can get your brand image in front of the right audience. Since the ads on a mobile screen are so prominent, you are also getting a good bang for your buck. Mobile users cannot ignore your ad on the screen in their immediate line of vision. But don't use mobile advertising only as a branding tool. Mobile can be more powerful than that. I always advise adding in the direct response component to your campaign to prove your ROI.

Direct Response via Mobile Advertising

As I have noted throughout this book, mobile is an effective direct response tool. There are six distinct ways that you can elicit a response from your customer (or soon-to-be customer) via mobile advertising: click-to-call, short message service (SMS) opt-in, email opt-in, location finder, click-to-video, and download content. Each of these can be used in campaigns for different reasons, but the bottom line is that each is quantifiable and trackable, so you can measure your response. This means you will know exactly which part of your advertising is working and which is not.

Click-to-Call

A brilliant use of mobile advertising for direct response is to get customers to call your business. They are already holding phones in their hands. In this method, users who click on your ad are sent to a landing page that provides click-to-call as an option. Customers simply click on the phone number and their phones start dialing. You can even make your ad a direct click-to-call tool by having users clicking on the ad itself, which will initiate the call. If you use this option, be sure your ad clearly states that this is what will happen. People will not appreciate being surprised if they dial a number unknowingly. Make sure that the number of callers and outcome of the call are tracked.

SMS Opt-In

With this option, users click on your ad and are taken to a page that allows them to send a text message to opt in to your offer. Any type of text message campaign, including a mobile coupon or a text message subscription, can work with this direct response opt-in. The process of having someone receive a text message with your location information will work well.

Email Opt-In

You can build an email list from your mobile advertising with an email opt-in page by using your ad to capture your customers' interest. Once they click through, users can read about the benefits of subscribing to your email list on the top part of the mobile landing page. Also provide the form for them to subscribe.

Location Finder

Your ad entices visitors to your site and to come into your store. Clicking the ad and going to a location finder page helps the visitors find you so they can actually send business your way. Remember that the most frequently sought information on mobile is location-specific information, so this is a powerful mobile advertising technique.

Click-to-Video

If you have video that can be incorporated into your campaign, this is an ideal option. Ads that include a "click to watch video" option have a higher response rate than the same ads shown without a link to video. Although you may be tempted, avoid showing a video commercial. You need to continue to provide value to your customers throughout the process. Instead, show something they will want to watch and put your call-to-action at the end of the video. You can also put a short (less than five seconds) promotion at the beginning of the video, if the content is compelling enough to keep viewers watching through the commercial portion of the video.

Download Content

You can entice users to download any wallpaper, ringtone, or application you provide. Just like the click-to-call option, click-on-the-ad can launch the download or stop at an info/permission page first. This is a powerful form of mobile advertising because many people like to get content on their phones.

Developing Customized Campaigns for Your Target Audience

To make sure you are putting your ads where they are relevant, work with your mobile ad networks (or your agency will do it for you) to choose the proper channels for display. Channels are groups of sites that offer the same kind of content: news, portals, sports, communities, or entertainment. Then the ad networks will work their behind-the-scenes magic to match your ad to a user even more carefully. It is best if you can match where your ads are displayed. Be sure to select the right countries for your ad campaign. If you don't sell internationally, be sure to place ads only in the countries that work for you.

Graphic Banner Ad Campaign

Banner ads have been around since the inception of the Internet, and the mobile version is not much different than the computer-sized one. But for each campaign, you'll need to create a banner ad in three to four different sizes to meet the needs of the variety of devices that will serve your ad. (Your ad network will give you specifics on the sizes you need to create.) The pricing for banner ads will be in the cost per thousands (CPM) model. Banner ads tend to get a better click-through rate (CTR) in mobile now. But this will not always be the case if the mobile web follows the Internet; banner ad CTRs are likely to decrease. On the other hand, clicking through on mobile can be a richer experience; there are more variations, and as just discussed, it does not mean you'll just go to a website.

Text Ad Campaign

As an alternative to placing banner ads on mobile websites, you can place text ads instead. These ads appear at the top of web pages in your chosen channels (topic), just as banner ads do; however, instead of paying every time your ad is seen (CPM), you pay on a pay-per-click basis. Text ad campaigns are not associated with search results; your ad is sent when someone is viewing a mobile website, much the same as a banner ad. The advantage of text ads is that you get what you pay for: Your results are tied into your advertising. Granted, you will lose the cool effect of your graphics, but you gain more control and accountability because it is trackable. Not only will you know how many people saw your ad, but you will also know how many took action because of it. If you are not getting the response you want, you can tweak your ad to make it better, and you don't have to pay for those who saw it without taking action. Pay-per-click is smart marketing and smart accounting.

Depending upon the ad network you're working with, you will only have about 35 characters to use for text ads, so you will have to be creative. Think fast, think fun, and cut to the chase. You don't have time for anything else, and neither do your customers. Remember, they are out and about. They're busy, and they will appreciate brevity. The following actions can increase your response rates for your text ads:

- Change your ad often, weekly if possible. On mobile, people like fresh and new, so do what you can to keep your ad energized. You can also rotate ads in your inventory so you have options.

- Make your call-to-action obvious and specific. People need to be told exactly what you want them to do, and they need a reason to do so. "Weekly specials offered" is not as clear and specific as "Click here to get weekly specials." In fact, "Click to get weekly 2-for-1 specials" is even better.

- Match your wording to your audience. Using a heavily abbreviated ad will work fine for teens who already use text abbreviations (such as "u" for "you" and "ur" for "your") but it doesn't work for people who are not used to such abbreviations.

- Many of the ad networks have ways to insert information in the ad that is specific to the user's phone. As an example, a person with a BlackBerry would see "Sports scores on your BlackBerry here," while the person with the Nokia would see the same ad as "Sports scores on your Nokia here." These types of specialization make the experience even more customized to the user and increases response.

- Create campaigns that tie in with holidays, seasons, breaking news events, or other dates that make your ad seem urgent. Users will know that after that certain holiday or event, the ability to click through will be gone. Plus, this makes your ad more relevant to their lives.

- Be sure to tease and tantalize. In as few words or as little space as possible, you want to entice the viewer to click through your ad. You want your ad to be compelling on the screen, so spend energy on this. You'll only have a second or two to grab the viewer's attention, and then the opportunity will pass.

- Make sure the page your customers will click through is the right page for the ad. Even more so than on the Internet, people will expect to find exactly what they were teased with in the ad.

- Use action verbs in your copy. If you're offering something free, use the word free in your ad. Both these techniques are proven to increase response rates.

Search Results Pay-per-Click

Search results pay-per-click (SRPPC) advertising appears when a consumer searches for a particular keyword. Advertisers only pay if consumers click on their ads. This type of pay-per-click is what Google AdWords and Yahoo! Search Marketing are all about. With mobile, the difference is that you have on-portal and off-portal searches. This gives you additional ad networks to launch your pay-per-click.

Pay-per-click has two basic components, and it is the art of doing both of them well that ensures a successful campaign. First, there is the ad itself. It must be well-written, and you must work on increasing your CTR throughout your campaign. Stay within the bounds of ethical advertising and best practices, and get your initial CTR as high as possible to create a good campaign. Next is your choice of where to show the ad. You will need to choose in which ad network(s) to place the ads. Then, within the network, you will choose the channels and sites where you want your ad to appear. Again, in mobile, it is important to be as closely matched as possible with the content that the visitor is seeing. If it is a sports site and you are advertising ladies' clothing, it is not going to work. At the same time, be responsive to new and different opportunities to see if the ad works.

What Is Mobile Publicity?

Mobile publicity is entirely different than the concept of using publicity to market your mobile campaign. It is about proactively putting your media message onto the mobile web so that reporters and journalists can find you when they need a resource or an expert as a source of information.

A mobile publicity campaign is much the same as an Internet publicity campaign: You want journalists, producers, and reporters who can cover your story in the media to find you. The difference is that they will find you via mobile and not their desktops.

When to Use Mobile Publicity as a Marketing Tool

If you have a publicity campaign underway, there is no reason not to have at least a mobile publicity kit available to any media person who may be searching on mobile for the right story or expert. You should also do what you can to ensure your mobile-friendly press kit is findable via mobile search. If your campaign is tied to breaking news, then consider having mobile advertising to support your mobile press kit.

How to Use Mobile Publicity: Best Practices, Tips, and Techniques

The Internet has certainly changed the way that journalists research stories and find experts to interview. Instead of leaving journalists dependent upon time intensive investigative research or tracking down contacts through publicists, the Internet puts the world's experts and information right at their fingertips. Journalists also find the mobile web just as helpful. To businesses, this means one more opportunity for mobile marketing. Mobile publicity is not only a way to drive more traffic to your mobile site; it builds up your publicity campaign.

Using a push campaign directly to journalists is not going to work. Mobile publicity is all about journalists being able to find an expert to interview on the mobile web or gathering information for a story while they are on the road. Having a mobile publicity campaign will be a veritable gold mine for folks who are experts on topics that have become breaking news. Reporters who need a quote quickly or an expert opinion will be likely to use the first credible source they can find. Make sure you're visible when a journalist is looking for you. This will mean being highly visible in mobile search engines and providing reporters with what they are looking for when they find you.

Creating a Mobile Press Kit

The first step to being accessible to media via mobile is to have a mobile-friendly media kit. Just as with your desktop-accessible online media kit, you want to include all the key components that journalists are seeking. Be sure to include press releases, a spokesperson bio, photos, video clips, audio clips, a background info page, statistics, ready-to-use quotes, and contact information. Host the online media kit on a mobile-friendly website. Also be sure that it is well organized for reporters. You will probably be using shorter versions of these media kit pieces in your mobile press kit, but be sure to provide access to the full information.

Using Your Mobile Media Kit to Get Media Exposure

A strong mobile search optimization strategy will be critical to your successful mobile publicity campaign. Make sure to follow all the steps outlined in this chapter's section on Mobile SEO. After all, it is likely that journalists will find you via mobile search. They will search for the keywords to find an expert, and you want them to find you. Be sure to have keywords such as expert, spokesperson, news source, interview, and media kit interwoven on your mobile media kit's home page. Working with SEO is a time-consuming process that you will have little control over, but make it part of your campaign strategy.

Having a mobile pay-per-click campaign ensures that you appear at the top of the search results when a media contact is doing a mobile search for your topic. This would be especially useful if there is a breaking news story that would have journalists scrambling for experts while they are on the move. This is a quick-response tactic over which you have total control. To set up a mobile pay-per-click campaign, follow the same steps outlined in this chapter for mobile pay-per-click but also include the words "Interview Expert Now" in your ad or something that makes it obvious that you are an expert that a journalist would want to find.

Tying in to Breaking News

If you have expertise that would be helpful to a reporter during a breaking news story, you should be ready to launch a pay-per-click campaign as soon as you become a good news source. As an example, let's say your company sells gold-panning equipment. When you hear on the news that a huge gold nugget was found in a river, you need to immediately launch your mobile pay-per-click campaign. Anytime the media wants to extrapolate or add on to the stories their competition is already running, it is time to introduce your big guns. It may or may not generate any media leads for you, but the beauty of pay-per-click is that you won't pay anything unless it does.

Chapter Updates and Online Resource Guide

Updates to this chapter and its related Online Resource Guide are available at www.mobilemarketinghandbook.com/Updates/Mobile Promotion.

The Online Resource Guide for Chapter 10 includes links for all sites listed in this chapter, as well as a Mobile Search Submission Action Plan, which is an Excel spreadsheet that lists the current mobile search engines and how to get your site listed in them. In the spreadsheet, you can track the date you submitted your site and the status of your submission.

Resources

The following resources are included to help you with further research and/or implementation of the ideas found in this chapter.

Mobile Search Resources

Deciphering Mobile Search Patterns: A Study of Yahoo! Mobile Search Queries, tinyurl.com/6ezxzx
Mobile Search Optimization, a White Paper by Resolution Media, www.mobilesearchoptimization.com/Mobile-SEO-White-Paper.pdf
Mobile SEO News (Bena Roberts), www.mobileseonews.com
Natural Search and Mobile SEO Blog (Bryson Meunier), www.brysonmeunier.com

Mobile Advertising Resources

Perry Marshall and Bryan Todd, *Ultimate Guide to Google AdWords* (Entrepreneur Press, 2006)

Mobile Ad Vendors

AdMob, www.admob.com
JumpTap, www.jumptap.com
Medio, www.medio.com
Mobile Marketing Association Mobile Advertising Guidelines, www.mmaglobal.com/mobileadvertising.pdf
Nokia Media Network, h217.162.2.145
Quattro Wireless GetMobile, www.getmobile.com
Third Screen Media, www.thirdscreenmedia.com

Mobile Publicity Resources

PressKit 24/7, www.247presskit.com
Peter Shankman, *Can We Do That?! Outrageous PR Stunts That Work—And Why Your Company Needs Them* (Wiley, 2006)

11

Social Networking and Mobile Campaigns

Over 800 million people worldwide will be participating in a social network via their mobile phones by 2012, up from 82 million in 2007.

—eMarketer

What Is Social Networking?

Chances are good that if you are 21 or older, you don't have a clue what social networking is or use it yourself. The chances are equally strong that if you are younger than 21, you do. According to Forrester Research, 80 percent of young adults (18–21) actively use social networking while only 20 percent of all adults (18 and older) do. So what is social networking anyway? It is a way for people who have similar interests or are in a relationship with one another to connect online or through mobile technology. A social networking site might be a website where people connect with other people they already know (such as former classmates or people who work in their company). It could also be a site where people submit reviews and recommend products and services to anyone who is interested in the same products and services. It might also be a discussion board where people who share the same hobby or interests can discuss their common bonds.

Social networking can involve people being notified via text message when their friends (or even friends of their friends) are nearby or whenever their friends choose to tell their network what they are doing. Or it could be a combination of all of these. The essence of social networking is how people connect virtually.

There are usually a variety of ways that users of a social network can interact, such as chat, instant messaging, text messaging, email, video, voice chat, file sharing, blogging, microblogging, discussion groups, and more. The idea is that through a social networking tool, people can have access to their social contacts through a number of communication methods. Communication is the crucial component of social networking. What is different about this communication is that it is often open and available to others, who can jump in if they want. So while a person-to-person email is private, most social networking communication is public.

The beauty of social networking and its value as a great marketing tool is relationship building. Social networking is all about creating relationships with your customers, future customers, colleagues, vendors, and anyone you want to get to know better. How different is this from old-fashioned push marketing in which you basically shove an ad in your customers' faces and hope they show up on your doorstep? I'm also struck by how similar it is to good old-fashioned getting-to-know people, with a bit of technology to facilitate the relationship. Social networking is simply something you have to experience to know how powerful it is. I encourage you to try it to see how it may work for your marketing needs.

When to Use Social Networking as a Marketing Tool

Chances are you will use social networking on the web as a tool for marketing your mobile campaign more than you will use mobile social networking as a marketing tool. But it is such a powerful marketing technique that you need to pay attention to this strategy.

Obviously, if your target market is young, you should be considering social networking in your marketing mix. After all, 80 percent of your market is already on board with the technology. If your target market is older (or technologically challenged), then you can probably set aside social networking as a primary marketing tool. After all, 80 percent of your market is not even using social networking. They may not even know it exists. But this will not be true for long. You might consider helping to introduce your market to social networking through education.

Social networking as a marketing tool works well for service-based or information businesses. After all, relationship building is a huge part of marketing these types of businesses as well. If you have a service-based business or sell information, you should definitely consider using social networking in your marketing mix. Your focus will be about building a presence and staying connected to your customers, colleagues, and vendors too. Even though your primary focus in social networking will be marketing your service, I highly encourage you to mix in personal information as well. Just as you get to know people personally in the offline world, you will do so online too.

Social networking can also work for retail or other types of brick-and-mortar businesses especially if you have an on-site "personality" (a popular or quirky owner, perhaps). The idea is that this person will be the face of your brand in social networking sites. Relationships can be built and attract a following within a social network if you do it right. As an example, if a local coffee shop on a college campus had a manager who was friendly, outgoing, and well-known by the students, that person could create a social networking presence and interact with customers in their social networking environment. This will work only if the right person is chosen.

One of my favorite uses of mobile social networking is as an extension of a physical event, such as a conference, trade show, festival, sporting event, or other occasion where people are gathered together. Mobile social networking adds a layer of connection to the event that makes it even better for those who participate. People can meet with one another easier, share on-site news, participate in polls or voting, or just chat about the event while they are there.

In all cases, you should only undertake social networking as a marketing tool if you have the time and patience to devote to networking. This is not an overnight-success type of marketing; it takes time and energy. If you are new to social networking, it will also take time to figure out how it works. Once you wrap your mind around this technology and build a good network of people who are doing the same, it will pay off.

How to Use Social Networking: Best Practices, Tips, and Techniques

I strongly recommend that you start using social networking yourself before you start thinking of using it as a marketing tool. The best practice in social networking is to participate, not advertise. Think twice about placing ads on social networks; ad response rates are notoriously low. Stick with building relationships and networking, not advertising. Participating as an individual is the most powerful way to use social networking. While you will be using it for your business, it is important to remember that people have relationships with other people, not companies.

Getting Started with Social Networking

To start social networking, find out what the most popular social networking sites are now and sign up. Check the Online Resource Guide for today's popular sites because they change quickly. As I write this, Facebook, Twitter, and FriendFeed are the leading social networking sites in the U.S., but that can change almost overnight. Technology moves quickly, and social networking is trendy. People hang out where everyone else is already hanging out, but this can change very quickly, especially among younger participants.

Once you know where everyone is spending time, choose one or two social networking sites and register yourself. Start participating. You are likely to find that one of these social networks will appeal to you more than others. That's OK as long as you are confident that your customers are on that network. Explore all aspects of the service and try various things. Don't worry that it won't make sense to you at first. If you are new to this, it can seem odd. That's normal. Once you are fully involved, it will seem like part of your normal day. Start with five minutes a day, and stick with it. Commit to trying it for at least a month or two.

Controlling Your Marketing Outcome in Social Networking

Before we go any further, I want to address a common question about how to control the outcome of social networking. Some marketing tools can give you total control. Take advertising, for example. You create the ad, and you decide when, where, and how it will be shown. You get exactly what you pay for with this tool. Other tools give you some control, such as publicity. With PR, you write up the release and choose how you want to position your message. But once it is in the hands of the media, it is up to them to decide what to do with it. Your press release can be ignored, it can be used "as is," or it can be the springboard for a completely different story that isn't what you wanted at all. Social networking as a marketing tool is more like PR than advertising. With social networking, you can choose your focus: Are you participating in a strictly business manner with a bit of personal stuff thrown in on the side (best for service-based businesses), or are you out to show how much fun you are (those quirky managers trying to attract students)? You can decide on your marketing message and act accordingly, but you can't make people want to socialize with you. It is as futile as a middle school student who announces, "I am popular." You can only control what you put out there and then hope it attracts the right people.

You will also see that many of the strategies, tactics, and tools you can use in mobile social networking require action by someone else. Your customers will need to take action for it to work as marketing. People who don't even know you or your business will need to take action, and this is out of your control. You can do everything right and still not get a good marketing response because it depends on others to take action. That said, social networking is a powerful tool, and you should try it to see if it works. Let's dive into some social networking tools.

Social Networking Sites

The meat and potatoes of social networking are the online sites such as Facebook, Bebo, and MySpace, where the majority of the interaction is done on the site itself when users log in and participate primarily from desktop-based computers. But each of these has a mobile component that lets users log into the site from their mobile and interact via the mobile web. Users can also have messages and updates from Friends sent via text message. It is possible for a person to be in 24/7 virtual contact with a huge network of people wherever they are. This is how the younger generation likes and expects life to be: connected. Regardless of their ages, people who have experienced social networking say it is a bit addictive.

If you are not currently using social networking, this concept can be completely foreign to you. It probably doesn't even register in your consciousness. As a 40-something myself, I found it odd to want to be connected to my family, friends, business colleagues, and acquaintances all the time. I'm used to interacting with business contacts in a business setting during work hours and personal contacts during nights and weekends. In my typical routine, the two sets of contacts would not intertwine or overlap. I was not used to anything else. To someone who is exposed to this much connection, it probably feels just as odd not to be so connected. Just think how much differently we use telephones than our grandparents. To them, the phone was a special tool used on special occasions. Now we call people just because we want to chat. To the younger generation, social networking is something they do because they always have been connected. They probably cannot imagine life without social networking. Increasingly, social networking is making its way into the mainstream and reaching a wider audience. Combining it with mobile makes it a one-two-punch knockout tool. If you can step into this world and effectively market your business, it may be the most powerful way you can use mobile in marketing.

Mobile Social Networking Sites

For the most part, people use mobile social networking sites when they have to and not because it's their preference. If they are out and want to check in on Facebook, LinkedIn, or MySpace, or post a tweet on Twitter, they'll use their mobile devices. But as soon as they are home and able to participate on their desktops, they do just that. There are also social networking sites that are designed primarily for mobile use with a secondary online component, such as Frengo, Flu, and Whirl. Marketing on them won't be that useful except as part of your overall social networking strategy.

But this could change as consumers become more integrated with mobile social networking.

Microblogging and Status Updates

A subset of social networking is called microblogging. Basically, this is a brief (140 characters) tidbit of information about yourself, what you doing, something you just discovered (a website, a new tool in your industry, or an article), a question you want to ask, a blog post you just wrote, or your thoughts about any particular topic. Obviously, it is micro because of the brevity of the information you can share. It is blogging because you post this information online or via your mobile device, and other people who follow you (or those who have agreed to get your information) will read it online or via text message. Again, it may not seem to make much sense on the surface, but it can be a powerful networking, relationship building, and branding tool.

The best way to understand this technology is to sign up for an account with a service such as Twitter or Jaiku and start participating. You can also use the Status Update feature in Facebook for the same effect. Try to find someone you know who is using it and read what they do. Go ahead and put in your own updates and see how it feels. At first, it may seem awkward and unusual, but I encourage you to stick with it. Once you reach a certain level of participation, it starts to just work. I advise sending a combination of microposts, some business and some personal. It helps to build relationships faster if you share some of your personal side, and it also is good not to get stuck in only posting personal items if you are trying to build business relationships.

Climb the Relationship Ladder with Microblogging

One great way to get to know people who are or can be influential is to befriend them in Facebook or follow their Twitter or Jaiku updates. You'll be surprised how much you can find out about people and how well you can get to know them through following their updates. For example, an acquaintance of mine was hoping to conduct business with a man she knew online. She signed up to follow his Twitter updates. One day, he posted that he was coming to her town. She immediately emailed him and set up an appointment to meet for coffee. He was happy because he had only one speaking engagement scheduled before his Twitter update. Once the folks who followed him knew he was coming, he received another booking. All this happened from sending out one quick microblog. This kind of relationship building is powerful. Even if all you do is follow a few people and occasionally answer their microblogs, you can start building a relationship. The next time they are speaking at a conference, you can introduce yourself. Chances are they will know who you are since you engaged with them using this technology.

Announcing Promotions through Microblogging

A business can offer coupons and other incentives to customers via microblogging. This would work best if you already know that your audience uses a particular service such as Twitter. You can announce (via signage, your ezine, newsletter, direct mail, Yellow Pages ad, or your website) that you have a Twitter coupon service. You simply suggest that people follow your Twitter feed, and they can get special discounts periodically. Then when you want, send out a coupon and be prepared for people to come in to redeem it. Obviously, this type of promotion works best when your target market knows what Twitter (or whatever service you use) is and uses it themselves. I can see this being particularly useful to nightclubs, coffee shops, restaurants, or other places that have drop-in traffic. It could even work for a busy hairstylist who is booked all the time. Those following her Twitter account would be alerted when there is an unexpected opening, hence helping fill the chair with happy customers.

Dell has two different Twitter deal feeds (www.twitter.com/DellOutlet and www.twitter.com/DellHomeOffers). The company sends out a few offers each month on Twitter that range from percentage-off discounts to announcements of refurbished computers that are an especially good value.

If you offer a coupon via Twitter, people will provide the coupon code and give you their phone numbers to redeem the offer. The point is that this gives you another way to get your offers in front of your customers. Here's an example of a Twitter coupon:

> Come into Joe's Coffee House, 123 Main St., by 5 pm on 2/15/09
> for two-for-one lattes. Coupon code: Blue12

Microblogging for the Niche-ly Famous

If you have people in your company who are "famous" within your business niche, you can use microblogging as a way to leverage their fame and increase their exposure, especially at industry events. One example from the self-publishing/book marketing world comes to mind. Each year at Book Expo America, the big industry trade show for authors and publishers, authors try to meet all the industry insiders who can help them with their books. These same industry insiders want to meet these authors because they are potential customers. At a trade show of 30,000 people, it is almost impossible to meet randomly. One year, John Kremer, an "A List" celebrity in self-publishing circles, announced to his email list that he would be sharing his location via Twitter throughout the trade show. People who signed up to follow him and had updates sent to their mobile phones had the inside track on where this industry insider was hanging out. It was a win-win situation. Kremer met more people who wanted to meet him, and these folks were able to gain access to their industry's celebrity. This brilliant strategy is often used by hundreds of people who attend the annual South by Southwest Music, Film and Interactive Conferences and Festivals in Austin, Texas. This can work for you if you are famous in your industry or want to be.

Mobile Social Networking Interwoven with Events

It may seem ironic that at an event where people are already "networking" face to face, they would find social networking a welcome addition. In fact, it is precisely because they are at the same event that social networking adds to their experience at the event. For example, people who follow each other on Twitter post updates about the event live from the audience, which is called live Tweeting. It creates a connected undercurrent of conversation at the event for the people participating in social networking.

At the 2008 Cinequest Film Festival, attendees used Mozes, a mobile marketing company that lets anyone make their campaign, promotion, or event more interactive by using the mobile phone and the web to vote for their favorite films using their mobile phones. As appropriate for a Silicon Valley-based film festival, attendees used Mozes's innovative live event features to text in their votes for the Audience Favorite Award and get up-to-the-minute updates and offers from Cinequest directly to their mobile phones. In addition to mobile voting, Cinequest used Mozes in innovative ways so that festival-goers had instant access to the most up-to-date information. Throughout the event, attendees could text via short code to join the Cinequest mobile list and receive announcements, schedule changes, and free ticket offers directly to their mobile devices. Additionally, each one of the individual films had its own Mozes keyword. When attendees sent a text of the film's keyword to the event short code, they immediately received the film's showtime, date, and venue directly on their phones.

Another example of mobile social networking at an event is when people who participate in a microblogging site such as Twitter use a special event code (e.g., #swsx) in their messages that groups all the microblogs relating to that event together. Everyone who is interested can then read all the comments that are made to the group in one location, such as www.twemes.com. Twemes also grabs photos that are uploaded in Flickr and Delicious with the same tags for a complete event experience. You can use a tool such as this for marketing by participating in event social networking. You will not only increase your exposure at or around the event because everyone else participating will see your brand repeatedly; you can also invite or remind people to attend your on-location events (trade show parties, trade show booth, lunches, and so on), and you can even extend special offers to anyone following you.

Mobile Photo Sharing

I recently saw an ad for a "YouTube ready digital camcorder." I was excited thinking that I had seen the first Internet-enabled camera. This particular camera was not actually connected to the Internet; it simply recorded video in the exact format that YouTube requires. It still required connecting to a desktop computer to upload the video. Then it hit me. Mobile devices with cameras in them are already connected to the Internet. A simple email to Flickr from a camera phone is all it takes to share photos with the world. Mobile makes connecting instantaneous through photos. Anyone with a camera phone can instantly upload and share photos. Through services like Flickr, Photobucket, SnapMyLife, and dozens of other photo-sharing sites, people can have a photo stream that is instantly shared with the world.

According to an internal survey by Fox Interactive Media (the News Corp. division that runs Photobucket), 80 percent of users who responded to the survey own camera phones, 36 percent use the camera every day, and 52 percent access the mobile web on their handsets. With use this pervasive, it is clear that mobile photo sharing is something that should be considered in your mobile marketing strategy.

Marketing with Mobile Photo Sharing

If you can figure out a way to get your customers engaged with your brand by taking photos and sharing them, you can market with mobile photo sharing. Punch Pizza, a Minneapolis pizza chain, launched a photo contest because it discovered that its customers were taking photos of the restaurant and pizzas and posting them to blogs. Originally, the pizza chain prohibited photos of its wood-fired pizza ovens because it didn't want its proprietary oven design to be stolen by competitors. When the pizza chain realized this particular policy was producing negative feedback from customers, the chain changed its strategy and launched a photo contest on Flickr. Grand-prize winners in each category were awarded a $500 dining card to Punch Pizza. Runners-up in each category received a $250 dining card. The restaurant also coordinated this photo contest with Facebook fan pages to take full advantage of the social networking tools. Throughout the contest, there were 286 entries, with tremendous feedback from customers who loved the idea. In this instance, the pizzeria took the cue from its customers who were already taking photos and leveraged it for marketing purposes. You can do the same for your business if you have something that makes sense for people to photograph and share.

For another example of mobile photo sharing for marketing, check out *Anthony Bourdain's No Reservations* photo stream on SnapMyLife.com. As he travels the world for the Travel Channel, Bourdain takes photos and shares them via mobile with followers on the mobile photo site. If you have a niche-ly famous persona and a sufficiently exciting reason for them to share photos while mobile, this is a technique that might work well for you. Another example comes from the scrapbooking industry. As the newest items are revealed at the industry trade show each season, there is a big rush for bloggers to get photos of the hottest items posted on their blogs. What if one of these bloggers used a mobile photo-sharing site instead and sent users a steady stream of new photos right from the trade show floor? This kind of marketing could be done by anyone with customers who are excited to see the latest and greatest items.

Campaign Ideas

To get your ideas flowing around what you can do with social networking, here are some campaign ideas you can try. More than any other tool, social networking is one you have to use in order to understand how it works:

- Market your social networking involvement off-line. Post signs in your place of business and alert people that you are participating in social networking. This can be as simple as posting a logo on Facebook, Twitter, or LinkedIn (or whatever site you network in) somewhere prominently with your profile page name. People who participate will notice it, and if they are interested, they will befriend you. This would be especially good to get people to sign up for your microblog coupons.

- If you think your audience might be interested in social networking but may not yet be up to speed with how it all works, add an article in your company newsletter to explain what social networking is and give a quick primer on what to do.

- Promote your social networking in your online environment. Put a badge or widget on your website. Use a signature line in your emails to encourage people to find you on the social networks.

- Keep your eyes and ears open. When the next MySpace or Facebook becomes popular, you want to be there. So listen and act on the news you hear. If you are active in social networking, this will be easy because it will start to come up in your conversations.

- Radio DJs can use a microblogging campaign to alert listeners to their on-location spots and get people to stop by. Instead of only having one way (on-air promotion to listeners) to promote an event, you can grab people who are not listening to the radio at all or who are listening to an alternate station by reaching them via mobile.

Chapter Updates and Online Resource Guide

Updates to this chapter and its related Online Resource Guide are available at www.mobilemarketinghandbook.com/Updates/SocNet.

The Online Resource Guide for Chapter 11 includes links for all sites listed in this chapter, as well as a list of social networking sites.

Resources

The following resources are included to help you with further research and/or implementation of the ideas found in this chapter.

Books

Rohit Bhargava, *Personality Not Included: Why Companies Lose Their Authenticity and How Great Brands Get It Back* (McGraw-Hill, 2008)

Joseph Jaffe, *Join the Conversation: How to Engage Marketing-Weary Consumers with the Power of Community, Dialogue, and Partnership* (Wiley, 2007)

Charlene Li and Josh Bernoff, *Groundswell: Winning in a World Transformed by Social Technologies* (Harvard Business School Press, 2008)

Geoff Livingston and Brian Solis, *Now Is Gone: A Primer on New Media for Executives and Entrepreneurs* (Bartleby Press, 2007)

Social Networks

Facebook, www.facebook.com
MySpace, www.myspace.com
Savor the Success, www.savorthesuccess.com
Twitter, www.twitter.com

Online Forum

Self-Starters Weekly Tips from Lynn Terry,
    www.selfstartersweeklytips.com/forum/index.php

Blogs

Chris Brogan, www.chrisbrogan.com
Nothin' But Socnet (Zena Weist), nothingbutsocnet.blogspot.com
Social Media Blogs at Alltop, socialmedia.alltop.com
Why Facebook? (Mari Smith), www.whyfacebook.com

Proximity Marketing

It has been a science-fiction dream for a long time. To have a phone that not only—and affordably—browses the Internet, but which is plugged into a geographically aware version of the net. Simms [Tomizone] says that, as you walk around, the phone will know where you are and bring alive your environment accordingly.

—www.blog.socialight.com/2007/12/26/
science-fiction-dream

What Is Proximity Marketing?

Proximity marketing is the distribution of marketing content associated with a particular place. It can be done by a business that is accessing a person's location through its mobile device's built-in GPS or by determining its position by the nearest cell phone tower, wireless access point, or other near-field communication technique, such as infrared beaming or Bluetooth discovery. Cell phone users can also do this by telling others (people, websites, businesses, or even signs) where they are located. Based on knowing the location of mobile devices, marketers can then communicate with (aka, market to) cell phones, laptops, and other devices located in a certain geographic area. The key ingredient is that the location of the mobile device figures prominently into the marketing.

When to Use Proximity Marketing as a Marketing Tool

If you are going to use a customer initiated strategy (when consumers decide to share where they are located and explicitly ask for location-based information to be shared with them) and you have a tech-savvy audience, you can proceed with proximity marketing using the techniques covered in this chapter. However, if you are thinking of going ahead with the type of location-based marketing that is an unwelcome surprise to the consumer, then I advise taking a step back to reconsider. Even though it seems like a marketing dream, proximity mobile marketing has the greatest possibility for being perceived as "creepy and invasive" by the consumer when the initial contact is not made with permission. While consumers know that their phones always know where they are, it is quite another thing to realize that their phones are sharing that information with outsiders who are trying to market to them. Proceed with caution when using proximity marketing, but don't be afraid to use it in the right circumstances. Be aware that some tactics in this chapter are more advanced techniques; either they require a more complex approach or they need specific hardware or software for implementation that is not yet widely accessible.

How to Use Proximity Marketing: Best Practices, Tips, and Techniques

As you know, the most important aspect of mobile marketing is getting your customers' permission before proceeding with your campaign. Just because technology allows you to automatically send a message to a phone that is close by does not mean that you should do so. Keep this in mind as you move ahead with proximity marketing. That said, all location-based marketing is not done by proactively reaching out to unsuspecting folks nearby. As always, the bottom line for success with location-based marketing is getting permission and providing value. Realize that an entire generation has lived with the Internet all their lives. They don't remember when going online was something unusual or even special. Soon they will also not think of the Internet as something to be accessed only from a fixed location, either at home or in a place that definitely has Wi-Fi. The Internet is everywhere and connected to everything.

Bluetooth Marketing

Bluetooth, a short-range wireless technology that essentially sets up a small wireless network between multiple devices, is one of the most exciting and controversial mobile marketing tools available. It is exciting because it offers the ability for multimedia files (ringtones, MP3s, graphics such as coupons or wallpaper, jpg, gif, and others) to be distributed to mobile devices quickly and without cost to transfer the files to either the business or the mobile user. This gives businesses and consumers what they want: a rich multimedia experience that doesn't cost anything to accomplish. It is also exciting because the marketing campaign is location specific, making it a uniquely mobile experience. It is controversial because the way the technology can be implemented is by making an initial outreach to a mobile device that is unsolicited. Here's how it works: Businesses using a Bluetooth marketing system can automatically send messages to any mobile device within a certain distance (usually about 30 feet) that has Bluetooth on and is open to being discovered. This initial message will give the consumer a "Yes" or "No" choice as to whether they want to accept a Bluetooth download. Proponents of Bluetooth marketing believe that since this first message is asking permission to send the Bluetooth message that it is a permission-based campaign.

But many others, including the Mobile Marketing Association, do not agree. This unexpected first message is what gives Bluetooth marketing the potential to be a sleazy marketing technique if used incorrectly. If you think I'm exaggerating, just read these snippets of sales copy (which have been changed enough to protect the companies that produced them but not enough to change their meanings) from websites selling Bluetooth marketing software: "The system can be used *covertly* by undercover personnel in situations where handing out written materials would either not be proper or permitted." Another site says, "Our software turns any computer into an advertising server that sends out your message 24 hours a day to *unsuspecting* cell phone users who come within 300 feet of your computer." Eye opening, isn't it? Not only is aggressive marketing like this ineffective, but it leaves a bad taste in consumers' mouths for interacting with businesses via mobile. For both those reasons, I do not advise marketing with this approach. The good news is that Bluetooth marketing can be handled with a more consumer-friendly approach, and this permission-focused method is exciting and offers some tremendous opportunities for value-based campaigns.

Establishing Mobile Zones

An effective use of Bluetooth in marketing is to build your campaign as a true opt-in version by reducing the minimum range for mobile devices to receive a message (maybe a few feet) and then marketing effectively so people choose to participate and receive a Bluetooth message. This would be establishing a clearly defined Bluetooth Zone that people are fully aware they are entering with the knowledge that if their Bluetooths are on and discoverable that they will receive a message. This permission-based concept will be welcomed by consumers. Of course, you will have to provide adequate value to them so they want to interact with your campaign. You can offer a range of things: coupons, audio files, screensavers, videos, games, business cards, ringtones, or pictures. Just remember the six things your customer wants from you via mobile: location-specific information, timely knowledge, things that make life easier, financial reward, entertainment, and connection.

Bluetooth Ideas to Be Used Within a Mobile Zone

Here are some ideas for Bluetooth Mobile Zones that work well in a complete permission-based scenario. I am noting this again because some vendors that use Bluetooth technology in marketing maintain that customers don't mind getting that initial message as a surprise. I disagree and suggest that businesses should only offer something via Bluetooth when the person who will get the offer will be expecting it.

- A restaurant can offer a Bluetooth coupon on its outdoor menu so that passers-by who stop to read the menu before deciding whether to go inside can be financially rewarded for doing so. The menu board would clearly indicate that it is a Bluetooth Zone so as people approached, they could be advised to turn on their Bluetooth and make it discoverable to get a message. If this campaign pushed the coupon offer to everyone walking by, it would not be permission-based.

- Concert-goers can get a picture of the performer they came to see, a teaser audio from an upcoming release, and a coupon toward buying the new CD. This Bluetooth Zone can be set up on the way into the concert, and fans could grab content on the way into the concert, but only if they approached the signs/kiosk to do so.

- At a trade show, a business can offer a video that demonstrates its product or service, a virtual business card, a brochure, or an audio message. Anyone who steps into the booth space can receive the initial message with the offer.

- Games, videos, or audios can be distributed in waiting rooms or places such as amusement parks, where there are long lines. Screensavers from the rides can also be offered, along with coupons for snacks or other items.

- Sporting event attendees can have the option of buying screensavers of the most famous players or the team logo and a coupon for buying a souvenir before they leave the venue.

- Museums can offer interactive information to go along with exhibits, including videos that give additional background on a particular exhibit, a game that makes the exhibit more interesting for kids, or even an audio guided tour that includes a gift shop coupon when they are done the tour.

- Tourist towns can offer a Bluetooth Zone at the visitors' center. Signs can be placed in businesses all over town reminding visitors to get their Bluetooth Guide to the city at the visitors' center. Coupons, audio tours, videos, scavenger hunts, and event calendars can also be given away from the Bluetooth Zone at the center.

- A shopping center can have a Bluetooth Zone positioned at key places such as the food court, each of the entrances, and the kids' play zones. Merchants at the mall can also offer a variety of coupons, events can be promoted, and even walking guides can be offered for mall walkers.

Surely you see the huge difference in businesses randomly reaching out to anyone with a phone nearby and offering people in close proximity the chance to choose to participate in something they find attractive. The offer that is ultimately made to consumers may be exactly the same, but the initial approach that proactively pushes it on them or attractively pulls them in is different. The results will be as dramatically different for both individual campaigns and mobile marketing in general. There is huge potential for consumers to be annoyed with pushed Bluetooth marketing, and they may not want to participate in anything via their mobile. This is much the same as how consumers quickly learned to give out temporary, fake, or not-often-checked email addresses to avoid aggressive email marketers. They will also quickly learn to leave their Bluetooths turned off or at least make their devices undiscoverable. So stick with mobile zones that entice people into participating for your sake as well as the entire mobile marketing industry's.

Interactive Signage

A big part of a successful proximity marketing campaign is interactive signage. Essentially, this is a sign that becomes interactive when people nearby turn on their Bluetooths to accept a message, send a text message to a short code noted on the site, or begin to browse on the mobile web because there is a mobile URL on the sign. Clearly, proximity marketing is not limited only to Bluetooth technologies. An excellent example of interactive signage is the Clear Channel Spectacolor HD digital billboard in Duffy Square in New York City. This sign features audio (people can listen to broadcasts from the billboard on their mobile phones), SMS messaging (people can send a text messages to and play games with the billboard), Bluetooth (audio and/or video can be downloaded from the billboard), Wi-Fi (the area is a free Wi-Fi hotspot), and streaming content (current news, weather, and sports are provided by CNN). You can see a demo of the sign at www.spectacolorhd.com.

Interactive signs don't have to be giant digital billboards. They can be as simple as a flyer posted with a text message call-to-action or a "For Sale" sign on a home that can deliver floor plan and pricing information. An interactive sign might be a table topper at a restaurant that has a voting campaign announcement or a stand-alone sign at a mall that provides alerts to people that they are in a mobile zone and gives them the information they need to decide to participate. The important component of an interactive sign is that it allows people to do more than just look at it, soak up the marketing message, and move on. The interactive part is what makes the sign a direct response tool. The art of creating interactive signs is something that you will want to master.

When creating an interactive sign, keep some of the following key principles in mind:

- Make your call-to-action obvious and exciting. Show the value that the person responding will receive.

- Be clear about what exactly the users will receive on their mobile devices or should expect via the interaction. It might be helpful to put the exact message that they can expect to receive on the sign itself.

- Include some graphic to indicate it is a mobile response you are asking them to perform. Until mobile response is completely common, you may have to introduce people to the concept that they should interact via mobile.

- Be sure to spell out any costs associated with their responses.

2D Bar Codes

Another tool that is used in proximity marketing is the 2D bar code, which is a two-dimensional bar code that mobile phone users can photograph or scan with their mobile phone cameras. Their bar code reader software automatically links their mobile browsers to a specific mobile website that was programmed into the bar code, or it sends a text message to them or even captures contact information into the address book of their phones. Basically, this is a form of shorthand for digital devices to read in such a way that saves consumers time inputting information into their phones.

These bar codes are widely used in Japan, and many people in the industry think they are soon coming to North America as well. The opportunity exists for smart marketing with them, but they are not common here yet for a few reasons. First, using them often depends on having a phone that has a full HTTP browser (a smartphone such as a BlackJack, Tilt, or BlackBerry) and can accept full software application downloads. Bar code reader software is not standard on most phones and will likely need to be installed by the user. Another big barrier in the bar code market in the U.S. has been that few consumers know what to do when they see a 2D bar code. If you want to market with 2D bar codes, be prepared to include adequate information to educate consumers on how to participate. Until we have a higher level of consumer understanding, wait a while before you construct an entire campaign around bar codes. It would be more effective if you use them in addition to a text message campaign or in addition to listing a mobile website URL.

You can create a 2D bar code easily with any number of bar code vendors, but you want to ensure you are using a very common bar code type so that the most people will have the bar code reader software on their phones. (It is much the same as creating an InDesign file, but if people don't have Adobe InDesign software on their computer, they can't open it.) You will likely also need to direct people to the site so that they can get bar code readers software, which is free.

A 2D bar code can be placed on product packaging so that additional information about the product is available with a click of your potential customers' camera. The code takes them to a mobile website that offers them more detailed information than is on the package. Bar codes can also be used in advertising so that a person reading the ad can just take a quick picture with her phone and find out all the details of what is offered in the ad, which are instantly sent to the reader's phone.

Image Recognition Marketing

Similar to bar code marketing, image recognition marketing requires a cell phone user to take a picture of an image (an ad, a book cover, a CD case, or a magazine ad). However, the similarity ends here. Instead of processing the image through software that has been put on the phone, the user sends the image to an image recognition company such as SnapTell, using email or short code. The information regarding the image is instantly sent back to the phone. *Rolling Stone* and *Men's Health* are using this technology in their magazines.

At Announcements

If your business model and customer base are open to the concept of social networking, a fun proximity-based tool to consider using is At Announcements (AT). Here's how it works: You sign up for a service (something like Brightkite) and so do your friends. Then throughout the day, you send a text message of your AT to the service with basically a quick text message that shares your location (where you are). This message is then instantly sent to all your friends who are signed up with the same service. Any friends of your friends who happen to be nearby also receive a text message (that's the social networking part). Through this service, all your friends know where you are located. Likewise, you know where all your friends are. One practical application may be to offer patrons of your restaurant, pub, or retail outlet discounts if they bring in additional customers while they are there. For a corporate example, the same type of offer can be made to someone visiting your booth at a trade show. If your booth visitors encourage colleagues to attend your presentation, some booth gift or financial incentive may be offered to the AT initiator for bringing new prospects into your booth.

Mobile Sticky Notes

When mobile social networking is mashed up with proximity marketing, it offers consumers the ability to leave virtual mobile sticky notes at practically any location. Here's how it works: Susie has lunch at a new Thai restaurant in her neighborhood. She likes it, and while she's waiting for the waiter to bring her check, she uses her mobile phone to write a mobile review at a site such as Socialight. A few weeks later, Tom, who lives in her area, is going to lunch. He pulls into a parking lot and sees several options where he could go for lunch, so he goes online to Socialight. Because his phone knows where he is, it brings up Susie's review as if it was just waiting for him. The next day Susie's friend (in real life and on Socialight) Linda goes into the same parking lot. Since she is Susie's friend in Socialight and has indicated she wants to know when any of Susie's virtual sticky notes are nearby, she gets a text message telling her Susie's thoughts about the restaurant. The mobile sticky note phenomenon may catch on with many people. It just depends on how useful it is in people's lives and how easy it is to use.

Your role as a business owner is to be remarkable enough that your customers want to leave virtual sticky notes about your business. You can also remind them to do so with strategically placed signs.

You can use mobile sticky notes in your marketing by creating a channel on Socialight about your topic. If you are a restaurant, create a restaurant channel. If you are a nightclub, go for a nightlife channel. Check in from places that are interesting to your target market. Include a sticky note at your business. You can also put up a sign in your establishment showing your positive mobile reviews. This can encourage more people to put up mobile sticky notes and to think about doing it in other places as well.

Permission and Data Privacy—Key Considerations

If you already have a customer loyalty program, you can add mobile marketing preferences to your customer profile that let customers indicate when and under what circumstances they are willing to accept your mobile offers or information. When you begin to add time, location, and personal preferences to your loyalty profiles, many customers see images of the Orwellian Big Brother and may opt out. Be clear about your data privacy and network security policies. There are digital identity standards and mobile application development tools, such as those offered by 5o9, Inc. that allow your customers to not only control their personal data (it lives on their device, not on your server) but determine when and how they will share that information. It is simply a browser plug-in that your web service provider can customize to your needs. From your customers' perspective, they are simply using the browser. The benefit of this approach is that location and preference data are available for a particular mobile marketing transaction without the need for you to store personally identifying data. If privacy or data liability is a concern for your business or for your customers, these new technologies are worth considering.

Chapter Updates and Online Resource Guide

Updates to this chapter and its related Online Resource Guide are available at www.mobilemarketinghandbook.com/Updates/Proximity.

The Online Resource Guide for Chapter 12 includes links for all sites listed in this chapter.

Resources

The following resources are included to help you with further research and/or implementation of the ideas found in this chapter.

Bluetooth Vendors

ILITOO, www.ilitoo.net

Bar Codes

BeeTagg, www.beetagg.com
KAYWA, www.kaywa.com
QMCODES, www.qmcodes.com
ShotCode, www.shotcode.com
Trillcode, www.trillcode.com
UpCode, www.upc.fi/en/upcode

Image Recognition

Snaptell, www.snaptell.com
SpyderLink, www.spyderlynk.com

Location-Based Social Networking

Brightkite, www.brightkite.com
Socialight, www.socialight.com

CHAPTER

More Mobile Methods

Mobile is one of the greatest technological and cultural transformations in history. It has revolutionized communication as we know it, and will have equal impact on how and when we gather and send information.

—Brian Fling, flingmedia.com

Trying to decide on the definitive tools and techniques of mobile marketing is a little bit like trying to get a 2-year-old to sit still. This chapter is a compilation of some important but unrelated concepts that need to be covered in a comprehensive book such as this; however, these topics don't need their own chapters. This chapter has been arranged in much the same way as the rest of Part 2: in order of most-applicable-to-use-now tools to the more advanced techniques. Early in the chapter are items that nearly everyone needs to be aware of for use in mobile marketing. Later in the chapter are the more advanced and technological stuff folks will want.

Mobile Email

A large percentage of people regularly check email on their mobile devices. Is your outgoing email easily read on a mobile device? Chilling question, isn't it? In the early days of email, everybody sent and received text-based emails. Then came HTML emails. Gradually over the years, as more email software started to read HTML-designed email effectively, more businesses started sending out graphic-filled emails. Now that so many people are checking email on their mobile devices (where multiple graphics might not even allow the email to open or render it just plain useless), it's time to think about offering an alternative. Currently, it is an email best practice to send messages in multipart MIME format. Don't worry if that sounds too technical; it just means that your email system will deliver your email in the best possible format for the device your reader is using to check email.

Much the same as with the mobile web, it may be best to offer your readers different content if they usually check their email with their mobile devices. Even if the phone will open up a long email, it doesn't mean that your customers will read it. Their mobile email services may not even download the entire message.

When you send a plain text email, be sure to keep your line length short (between 60 and 65 characters is standard). If you know you have a lot of mobile email readers, you can make your text email even more compact. Also keep in mind that on a mobile email system, your readers may not see who the sender is. It is helpful to include a note in your subject line to indicate who the sender is. However, your subject line is going to be even more important, both real estate-wise (you have fewer characters to display) and content-wise (your subject line needs to be provocative enough for someone to open an email on their mobiles).

Mobile Email List

If you know a large percentage of your readers open their email via mobile, you can create a special mobile email list. On your site where visitors go to subscribe to your email list, you can offer a special mobile list that is especially designed for a mobile device. (It could be your m-zine instead of your ezine.) The mobile version of your email can consist of headlines overall and short paragraphs that link to a mobile website for further reading. It can also include a way for readers to send a reminder to themselves to read a full-size version later.

Mobile Billing and Payment Options

It would be impossible to adequately cover m-commerce (buying and selling of goods and services via mobile) in the scope of this book, but I would be remiss not to mention ways that mobile users can pay for products or services with their mobile and ways you can collect those payments. Downloadable items will almost always be purchased through and billed by the carriers. The carriers stay in charge of downloadable payments for two reasons: 1) to protect their customers from unscrupulous vendors, and 2) to protect their share of the revenue stream that downloadable content brings to the bottom line. If you are going to sell downloadable content, you will be sharing part of your revenue with carriers, and all billing will be done through them. Even if you were to go through a site that will help you create and sell downloadable content, you will only get a percentage of the profits, and they will handle all billing.

If you are going to sell anything that is not downloadable, such as physical goods (books, sporting goods, food, tickets for an event, clothes, and so on), then you can accept payment via mobile using one of the mobile payment providers listed here. Before you dismiss selling physical goods via mobile, consider that Juniper Research reported in 2006 that U.S. consumers spent an estimated $480 million on physical merchandise using their mobile devices, and the U.K-based research firm expects this figure to exceed $1.9 billion by 2010. The following vendors can help you set up your mobile payment gateway.

PayPal Mobile

PayPal users can set up a mobile PayPal account so that anytime they are on a site or see an ad for something they want to buy via their mobile, they can do it. This would be perfect for selling tickets to an event. Just put the PayPal logo on the marketing materials and show people how they can register and pay for the event immediately.

ShopText

ShopText is a mobile commerce and promotions company with a software platform that transforms any ad into a point-of-sale opportunity. ShopText technology creates a secure, direct-to-consumer marketplace where consumers can shop, sample, and save. Your customers can sign up with ShopText by signing up online, entering their credit card information, and then activating their phones. Each time they want to buy from a ShopText vendor, they can just text the keyword from your ad and enter their pin codes. Bingo, they just ordered with their phones.

Bango

Bango is one of the biggest mobile payment gateways that can collect money for you worldwide through your customers' phone bills, credit cards, or PayPal accounts. Bango has a free starter package that allows you to sell up to 10 products and get 20 percent of the revenue from your sales. Its pricing ranges up to $1,599 per month, and for that, you get more services and can keep up to 90 percent of your revenue. Bango is an option for those who sell worldwide or are a major brand.

mPoria

I saved mPoria for last because it is technically not a mobile payment program but a complete m-commerce provider. Its GoMobile! service is a turnkey m-commerce solution that enables retailers to build, customize, and monitor a complete m-commerce site easily and cost effectively. If you want to sell physical products via mobile, mPoria is the tool you need. You can open a mobile store in minutes, and you can sell your wares almost immediately at a surprisingly affordable investment.

Mobile Widgets

To consumers, mobile widgets are simply small graphic files that can be downloaded onto their phones. When consumers click on the widget, it launches an application, opens a website, starts a game, triggers a video, or sends whatever the widget creator decided. To marketers, widgets are the opportunity to have space on the mobile screen and be closer to their customers. As with all mobile, your widget needs to provide specific and appealing value or no one will download your widget. Some of the most popular are ones associated with major brands (Wikipedia, *Wall Street Journal*), fun games (Suduko, Memory Game), weather, news, stock quotes, and more.

All widgets are not created to work on all phones. Some (WidSets) work on Java-enabled mobile phones; others (Yahoo! Mobile Widgets) work on iPhones; some on Windows Mobile devices and Nokia S60 series. You get the point: Widgets are cool but certainly not universal. This is one good reason to know which headsets the majority of your mobile site visitors use so you can focus your efforts on the type of widgets most of your users can access. By using mobile-specific analytical tools as described in Chapter 6, you will know this important piece of data.

Widgets as a marketing tool have great potential if they are the right match for what you offer. People only get widgets that appeal to them for their own reasons. You won't be able to get away with a widget that doesn't provide value to the person who is going to put it on his mobile device. Check out the following widget sites and see what makes sense for what you do. You'll either start getting ideas, or you won't. Either way, you'll know if widgets are a good option.

Tips for Creating Successful Mobile Widgets

According to Yahoo! Mobile (www.mobile.yahoo.com/developers/ tips), the following specific tips can be used to create successful widgets:

- Tap into mobile user passion points. Hit on a passion point, content, or service that mobile consumers want and need while they are on the go.

- Provide personalization and customization. The best widgets provide updated information based on users' customized preferences. Let users customize your widget so they only get the stuff they want.

- Keep things simple—don't try to incorporate too many features into one widget. You can always build more than one widget.

- Optimize for a mobile experience. Be mindful when designing your widget that it will be on a smaller screen and that network speeds will be slower on a mobile phone.

- Keep it fresh. The most regularly used widgets are those that constantly provide new, up-to-the-minute information to users.

iPhone Application Development

There is no doubt that the Apple iPhone has changed the mobile industry and that there are opportunities galore for developing websites and applications for it. As the most voracious consumers of the mobile web, iPhone users are a good target for specific applications. In Chapter 9, I discussed building iPhone-specific websites, and here I am covering applications—software or widgets that run on the device. Since all iPhone applications (not widgets, though) must be provided through Apple, your application must fit into one of the following categories:

- Calculations

- Entertainment

- Games

- News

- Productivity

- Search tools

- Social networking

- Sports

- Travel

- Utilities

- Weather

To be clear, application development is not a do-it-yourself job unless you are a software developer. To download the iPhone software development kit (SDK), you need to sign up as a Registered iPhone Developer and be running an Intel processor-based Mac on Mac OS X Leopard. If you meet those requirements or are willing to hire someone who is, then you can dive into iPhone development.

Video and Audio

Audio and video have huge potential in mobile. User adoption and a phone's ability to handle it are not significant enough to warrant launching full campaigns around it. Of course, this will change quickly. If you can think of a situation where your customers are mobile and need or want something that you can provide with a video, then you should consider mobile video marketing. Here's how it would work: Your customers can see your other marketing (maybe a sign, a billboard, or a flyer, or hear you on the radio). You can offer them a short code; they can reply to get a link to a mobile video. It can work for cars, houses, or other big ticket items that you are willing to invest in to promote via mobile. Consumers are also willing to deal with the technical details of getting a video.

Mobile video will also be big in user-generated content. If you can think of ways to get users to create a mobile video and share it, you might be onto something. But be aware that user-generated TV commercials are already considered to be old news, so you might find that as quickly as user-generated mobile comes in, it will go out again.

Mobile TV Advertising

MobiTV, the nation's largest mobile TV network, had 3 million subscribers at the beginning of 2008. Granted, this is a small percentage of the overall mobile phone users, but it is still 3 million people, 82 percent of whom are between the ages of 18 and 39, and the remaining 18 percent age 40 or older. These subscribers (67 percent male and 33 percent female) love television, are highly mobile, technophiles, trend setters, and mavens who drive tech purchases, both within corporations and among their friends. If you are trying to reach such a target market and have a significant budget, you can look into adding MobiTV advertising to your marketing mix.

Mobile Marketing Awards

When you create your amazing mobile marketing campaign and get the results you were dreaming of, enter your campaign in the Mobile Marketing Association's Mobile Marketing Awards (MMA Awards; tinyurl.com/mobile awards).

Chapter Updates and Online Resource Guide

Updates to this chapter and its related Online Resource Guide are available at www.mobilemarketinghandbook.com/Updates/More Mobile.

The Online Resource Guide for Chapter 13 includes links for all sites listed in this chapter.

Resources

The following resources are included to help you with further research and/or implementation of the ideas found in this chapter.

Mobile Email Resources

AWeber, www.aweber.com
Blue Sky Factory, www.blueskyfactory.com

Mobile Payment Resources

Bango, www.bango.com
mPoria, www.mporia.com
PayPal, www.paypal.com
ShopText, www.shoptext.com

Mobile Widget Resources

Mobile Widgets White Paper, www.littlespringsdesign.com/resources
Plusmo Mobile Widget: Publish Your Own Widget,
    www.plusmo. com/create/publish.shtml
Sexy Widget, www.sexywidget.com
WidSets, www.widsets.com
Yahoo! Mobile Widgets, www.mobile.yahoo.com/developers

iPhone Application Development Resources

Fling Media, www.flingmedia.com
iPhone DevCenter, developer.apple.com/iphone

Articles

Brian Fling, "Mobile 2.0: Design and Develop for the iPhone and Beyond,"
    www.mobilemarketingprofits.com/111
Craig Hockenberry, "Put Your Content in My Pocket," A List Apart,
    www.alistapart.com/articles/putyourcontentinmypocket

Mobile TV Advertising

MobiTV, www.mobitv.com/contact/Ad_Deck_r4.pdf

Moving Ahead
in Mobile

Finishing this book was difficult. It wasn't just about getting it done, although my family and friends can attest that was certainly part of it. The difficult part was deciding how much to include. Mobile marketing encompasses so many strategies, ideas, techniques, and tools, and I wanted to include as many of them as possible while still providing enough depth and information. It was also difficult because of all the new enhancements to technologies and the many innovative offerings from vendors (even the carriers were starting to offer unlimited packages) that occurred while I was writing. Frankly, there were days when I thought that writing a book about mobile marketing campaigns was an impossible task. And, of course, none of these wonderful improvements will stop just because I sent my manuscript to the publisher.

By the time you read this, more exciting things will have happened in mobile marketing. However, nothing will change the fundamental principles covered in this book. Customers will always need to find value in engaging with mobile marketing. Mobile initiatives will always need to be integrated into other marketing mediums to succeed. Campaigns will need to be launched and tracked with the attention to detail that mobile requires. Your choice of what to do in mobile is only limited by your creativity and your willingness to try something new.

The unlimited pricing packages now hitting the U.S. will surely help expand the mobile market. As people begin to sign up for those all-encompassing plans, they will want more powerful mobile devices to take advantage of what they are paying for; they will also expect to find plenty to do. This is where you come into the picture. Give them something meaningful to do with their new devices and all-inclusive plans. You'll be glad you did.

On that note, I urge you try mobile marketing, see what happens with your customers, and find out what works and what doesn't. Until you try mobile, you will be missing out on the newest and most powerful marketing tool of our time. It is up to you to dive in and make something happen. You may be surprised at the great response you get. Since you will have read the entire book, you'll know how, and you'll also know who can help you. I am certainly one of those people.

Through the Online Resource Guide at www.mobilemarketinghand book.com and my blog, MobileMarketingProfits.com, I will keep you updated on what is new in the industry and give you access to fresh ideas in mobile. Feel free to contact me with questions, offer suggestions, and share your success stories. You can email me directly at kim@mobilemarketing handbook.com, and I will be happy to point you in the right direction and/or offer solutions for your needs.

Thank you for coming along on this journey through the world of mobile marketing. It is only the beginning for both of us. Go forth and market with mobile. Keep me posted on how it is turning out for you.

Putting Mobile
into Context

While many books in the mobile marketing genre include information about mobile marketing, the technologies that power mobile, and the philosophies behind marketing with mobile, I have stayed focused on how to carry out a mobile marketing campaign. However, there are some important concepts about mobile, specifically as they relate to the value provided to the consumer that may be helpful for you to know as you proceed into mobile marketing.

The 6 M's

To fully understand mobile as a marketing tool, it is helpful to consider a broader view of the mobile industry and how companies develop the tools and technologies that consumers use. Mobile giants including Ericsson, Orange, Motorola, Nokia, NTT DoCoMo, T-Mobile, Vodafone, and others adopted a service creation tool called *The 6 M's* that was introduced by Tomi T Ahonen, Joe Barrett, and Paul Golding. These six attributes are important to users in their mobile experience. The 6 M's are important to you as a mobile marketer because these are aspects of mobile use that the industry players are using to make product creation decisions and evaluate mobile service concepts. The 6 M's are what virtually all mobile applications, services, and devices are built around and how they are compared. Even though it seems a bit technical, it is worthwhile to understand this foundation concept from these industry leaders.

The 6 M's (according to Ahonen in *Mobile as 7th Mass Media Channel*) are the following:

1. Movement

2. Moment

3. Me

4. Multi-User

5. Money

6. Machines

All major players in the mobile industry build billable services for mobile using the 6 M's theory. It is the only comprehensive mobile service development tool, so you should be familiar with it. The basic concept is that each application, mobile service, or mobile device has each of these attributes in varying degrees. It is a recipe or formula for mobile success based on including each of these 6 M's in a certain proportion. Let's examine each of them briefly.

Movement

The first M is the attribute of mobility. Movement comes into play when you consider where someone is using his or her mobile device and integrate that accordingly into your offering. This is what makes mobile web use different from desktop Internet access. A person needs a reason to go online with his or her mobile device instead of the desktop, and that reason depends on location, specifically if it is not within reach of his or her desktop computer. The more you can incorporate where people are when they are interacting with your company via mobile, the more successful you will be.

Moment

The second M is for moment, which is all about expanding the concept of time. As it is explained in *Mobile as 7th Mass Media Channel*, "Moment includes catching up on past time (yesterday's sports scores) or postponing time (putting a person on hold) as well as managing time (calendaring)." Think about your business and how your customers can get value from your company through expanding time. What is it that they want from you as it relates to their time?

Me

Me is the third M and refers to the personalization and customization of the phone. From the moment users choose a ringtone, they are personalizing their mobile devices, and this customizing never seems to stop. From the accessories chosen to the choice of applications used to the sites accessed, mobile device use is about one person: me. Anything you can offer that is personalized or specifically customized has a better chance of being well received than anything that is designed for everyone.

Multi-User

As personal as the mobile device is, its power lies in the fourth M, which is all about the community the device can help build and help the user interact with. Chat and user-generated content are the tip of the iceberg as far as this M is concerned. Multiplayer mobile games, mobile social networking, and anything else that helps users collaborate with each other via mobile falls into this category. If there is anything you can offer that helps your customers belong to a community they wish to belong to, do it.

Money

The fifth of the 6 M's is the money attribute, which encompasses everything from payment systems to let users make purchases with their mobile devices to loyalty programs and third-party payments such as employers' directly depositing paychecks to mobile or parents paying allowance via mobile. All money-related functions in your mobile marketing campaign should be simple and secure.

Machines

The last of the 6 M's is machines, which is all about the gadget itself. What can the machine do? From the actual buttons and knobs to the function that the machine can perform, this M is exciting. Imagine your phone as your personal remote control device to virtually everything from your TV and the lights in your home to your robot. While it is not likely you will be building or offering mobile devices, keep in mind what your customers are using to interact with you.

Examining the 6 M's in more depth is a worthy venture. For more details, check out Ahonen's book.

How Is Mobile Different than Other Marketing Methods?

It is important to understand how mobile is different than other marketing so that you can take advantage of the full power of the medium. As with any tool, it is best to use mobile for its intended purpose and to use it correctly.

As an example, you can get a screw into a piece of wood with a hammer, but it is certainly not the most efficient way to do it. If you can see mobile for what it is—the seventh mass media—you will be able to create much more dynamic and successful mobile marketing campaigns.

Understanding Mobile as the Seventh Mass Media

Probably the biggest mistake that businesses and marketing professionals make in marketing with mobile is that they don't see mobile any differently than any of the other media they are already using to market. Many see it as a small TV or a dumb/slow computer and plan their marketing along those lines. But it is crucial for a business that wants to market smart with mobile to see it as an entirely new media: the seventh mass media. To understand that concept, we need to backtrack a bit and understand the first six mass media and how each subsequent newcomer changed the forerunners. Again, this is examined fully in Ahonen's book, but it is such a crucial foundation to a successful mobile marketing campaign that I'm including an overview here, with permission from Ahonen.

We've come a long way from the first mass media: print. In the mid-1400s when Johannes Gutenberg improved the printing press and mass printing became available, it revolutionized the world. Instead of only a handful of literate people who could participate in the world's knowledge, literacy became commonplace. Large groups of people read the same thing, and information was shared on a wide scale for the first time. The common man found tremendous power since print allowed political influence by the masses, put religious texts directly in the hands of people that reduced the power of the church, and provided a way for literature to be shared easily.

It was not until the late 1800s (400 years later) that recording became the second mass media. This allowed music and books to be shared more universally, but it did not wipe out print as the first mass media, which some people believed that it might. This is important because every time a new media comes along, people think that it will wipe out previously existing ones; it never does. There were several generations who lived with print as their only mass media.

The third mass media was cinema, which came along in the early 1900s, making the turn-of-the-century population the first to live with three sources of mass media. The cinema brought multimedia (audio and video) to the world as well as the first pay-per-view business model. Many thought that the invention of the cinema would cause print and recordings to disappear. But that didn't happen. All three media forms grew and thrived.

Scarcely 10 years after cinema came radio, the fourth mass media. Radio brought "streaming" content delivery where a person has to listen live or miss the content. This was also the first media that was broadcast and received simultaneously by all listeners. Everyone who tuned in heard exactly the same thing at exactly the same time. Families gathered around the radio to listen together to the news, stories, and music. You begin to see how quickly new mass media comes into people's lives, especially since the children of this time period are now in their 90s or have already passed on. These folks have seen the greatest changes in technology of any generation so far.

In the 1950s, TV became the fifth mass media and began to shift and change the other media. In some cases, the new media completely cannibalized features of the old. For example, newsreels (short news documentaries) were played in movie theaters until TV news shows took over. Can you imagine going to the movie theater today to find out what is going on in the world? Today, in the time it takes to get in your car and drive to the theater, you can find dozens of news channels on TV for the news. TV also changed how we consumed content: We watched instead of listened. Because there were only a few channels to watch and only one TV per household, families watched the same shows together at the same time. Advertising on network TV was successful because only a few brands were available for consumers and a large percentage of the population saw the advertising. As a teenager in the 1980s, I witnessed the birth of MTV and heard dire predictions about TV finally killing off radio. While the widespread use of TV changed how we focus on radio (we listen while we're at work or in the car, and families certainly don't gather around to hear a radio show), it did not wipe radio off the face of the planet. And video did not kill the radio star as the first song played on MTV suggested. But it did change how someone became a star; music videos became the fastest road to stardom, not radio play.

TV shifted the other media but didn't really bring anything new to the table. Video images already existed in the cinema; TV changed where these images were viewed. Broadcast already existed with radio; TV just switched the broadcast from audio-only to a multimedia experience of audio and video. Even so, TV dominates the mass media. With the advances in technology, such as high-definition TV and flat-screen TV monitors, it is clear that this media is squeezing cinema even more. We can sit at home on a cozy couch and watch a movie with the family instead of going to the theater and sitting in a cold room with strangers who may talk through the entire movie. (At least you can tell your own family at home to shush.) I can see a future without movie theaters at all. Drive-ins are already gone, but that's another story.

The sixth mass media, or the Internet, came into play in the mid-1990s. What is unique about the Internet as a mass media is that "it is capable of replicating all of the other five previous media," according to Ahonen. You can read books, newspapers, and magazines online, you can watch broadcast TV and listen to radio online, view movies and listen to recordings (podcasts, anyone?), all on the Internet. All five other mass media are also available on the Internet.

Does this mean that all the other media will disappear? Of course not. Will people curl up with their laptops on the beach to read the latest novel? No. But printed newspapers are declining and will likely someday go the way of the newsreel. At some point, it will be inconceivable that we used to have 12-hour-old news printed and delivered to our doorstep just as it is to us now that people went to the movies to catch a newsreel. The content will still be there, but consumers will consume it differently, more quickly, and from a wider range of sources. Evidence of that can be seen when popular bloggers are now competing for readers head to head with newspapers and achieving comparable readership numbers. Amateur videographers are now able to produce and market their own shows that often get viewership figures rivaling some cable TV shows. Consumers have become their own media sources.

In addition to replicating the other five mass media, the Internet as a mass media brought a threefold functionality to the world: interactivity, search, and mass ability to contribute in a significant way. Never before had a mass media allowed for interactivity so quickly. Yes, viewers could write to a TV station to express their views, Letters to the editor have been printed for years, and radio stations have fielded callers for decades. But the Internet blew interactivity wide open. From consumer reviews to article comments to video ratings, anyone can interact with almost anything that is produced online immediately. The ability to search quickly and easily through an almost infinite amount of data has certainly shifted things. I can't even remember the last time I used the printed Yellow Pages, in which I have to figure out what category I should use to look up a service instead of just typing what comes naturally to mind. My daughter can't even fathom doing homework research without the Internet as a resource.

Without a doubt, the biggest change in mass media with the Internet is the ability for the masses to become contributors. When Gutenberg first fired up the presses and printed the Bible, it was one of the few texts available to be printed. Now so many bloggers are blogging, podcasters are recording, videographers are creating their own shows, and people are creating their own radio programs that *Time* magazine named user contributors collectively as Person of the Year in 2006. The masses are the media now. We are not just sitting around waiting for whatever is sent down the pipeline to us. Through the Internet, consumers have become the media. Clearly this change is what makes the Internet so powerful as a mass media and changes the face of mass media as a whole.

As powerful as TV was to change in the world and as seemingly unbelievable as the changes were that the Internet generated, these pale in comparison to the power of mobile as the seventh mass media. Remember that mobile is not just about phones; it is about any device that can do what other mass media does but in a mobile environment. When you combine the fact that this can replicate all other forms of mass media and is the most widely owned and used media tool in the world, it becomes obvious how powerful it is.

If you consider the adoption rates of mobile, it is simply astounding how prevalent mobile device use is around the world. Over half the population of the planet has a mobile phone. In many countries, the adoption rate is more than 100 percent. In the U.S., that rate is 80 percent; in Canada, it is 60 percent. Almost everyone has a mobile phone these days.

In addition to being so widespread, mobile as a mass media is extremely personal. Everyone knows that hundreds of thousands of others are reading a newspaper and the ads are targeted only by geographic vicinity. Virtually any ad could apply to any of the readers within a metro area. Everyone knows that millions of others are watching a TV show (and probably skipping through the commercials on their Tivo, too), and the ads are targeted to the general demographic that is watching the show. On mobile, it is possible to make sure that ads are precisely geographic and specifically personal. For example, a person who has done a mobile search for a specific restaurant in the past can see an ad for that restaurant when reading an online news story on his phone in a nearby automotive repair shop waiting area. The woman right next to him reading the same news story might see an ad from a nearby shoe store where she has a loyalty card that is tracked through her mobile device. Meanwhile, the busy mom across the room could be getting a text message coupon from a fast food eatery where she frequently takes her kids when she needs a quick meal on the go. Compare that to the TV that is also on in the waiting room. All three of these people see the exact same advertising regardless of whether it applies to them personally. There is no other media that can reach all these people with the message that is exactly right for them at the exact time that works for them while they are geographically located close enough to take action.

Another reason that mobile is so powerful as a mass media is that it is always carried and always on. People have their phones with them at work, while they are running errands, when they are out to dinner, while they're at the gym, and just about everywhere else they go. Surveys have shown that 60 percent of the population even sleeps with a phone by their beds. This is not to say that all these times are open opportunities to market to your customers; it just shows that the media is highly interwoven into the daily lives of people and makes the mobile device extremely powerful as a mass media tool. And because mobile replicates all other media, it leaves other media vulnerable to changes in use. If people can easily and conveniently replace with mobile what they currently get through other media, they will. When it becomes simpler to get the exact news you want (and none of the stuff you don't) delivered directly to you wherever you are and whenever you want to read it, this is likely to replace printed newspapers.

The last thing that makes mobile so powerful is that a payment mechanism is built into the device. A person interacting with your company via mobile has the ability to make a purchase immediately with the click of a button. It no longer requires an extra step to get the purchase. It is quite likely that our mobile devices will become our primary method of payment. Someday it will seem unusual not to pay for most of our everyday purchases with our cell phones.

The bottom line about mobile as the seventh mass media is that it will be integrated into the lives of consumers so quickly that we will likely be shocked at how fast. And just like generations that came before us, we are probably watching the younger folks take to it like a fish to water. After all, they don't know life without any of these tools and without each individual having the power to be their own media outlet. As a marketer, you just need to stay on top of how to use this media channel.

Glossary

Additional glossary terms can be found at www.mmaglobal.com/ glossary.pdf.

2D bar code. A graphic image that can be photographed by a cell phone camera and causes the cell phone to take an action embedded in the graphic, such as providing details on a specific product. Requires software to be already operating on the phone.

abbreviated dialing codes. A two- or three-digit code that is dialed after the # sign. Allows callers to dial quickly into a campaign without using a 10-digit phone number.

ad blindness. The phenomenon in which consumers cease to notice ads because the ads are always in the same place or are unnoticeable for whatever reason.

application providers. The official industry term for text message companies.

Bluetooth. A wireless short-range communications tool that transmits data over short distances from fixed and/or mobile devices.

brand awareness campaign. A marketing campaign that is designed only to increase awareness of a brand name and not set up to elicit direct response.

call-to-action. A specific action that marketers want a consumer to take as a result of their marketing efforts.

click through. The act of a website visitor who clicks on an ad and gets to the page that is being advertised.

click-through rate (CTR). The percentage of clicks an ad gets in relation to the number of impressions. If 100 people see an ad and 3 of them click on the ad, the CTR is 3 percent.

click-to-call. A link on a mobile web page that when clicked initiates a phone call.

click-to-video. A link on a mobile web page that when clicked initiates a video to play on a mobile device.

connection aggregators. Companies that technologically connect text message companies (application providers) to cell phone carriers.

conversion. Percentage of people who take a suggested call-to-action compared to how many were originally offered the option. If 100 people see the call-to-action and five of them do it, the conversion rate is 5 percent.

corporate data plan users. Cell phone users who are given a phone by their employer and have access to a data plan.

cost-per-thousands (CPM). Standard advertising rate of charging/paying for how many thousands of people view an ad.

data plans. Pricing plans charged by cell phone carriers for mobile web access, text messaging, GPS, and other uses in addition to standard phone calls.

double opt-in. The process of consumers' agreeing to a confirmation message that they want to receive a text message or email subscription.

guerrilla marketing tactics. Low or no-cost marketing tactics that are often implemented at a grassroots level.

interactive signage. Signs that become interactive when a direct response mechanism is added to them via mobile marketing.

keyword. In text messaging, the word that is sent to the short code triggering the campaign.

loyalty program tracking. Customers keeping track of their purchases at a certain business to receive a reward for their purchases.

media worthy. Information that is worth the attention of the editorial media and not just a sales pitch, which is more applicable to an advertising department.

microblogging. Blogging in short snippets using a third-party service such as Twitter, Pownce, or Jaiku.

microposts. The actual blog posts of microblogging.

mobile coupons. Discounts or financial incentives offered via mobile devices. Usually delivered by text message.

mobile-specific analytical software. Software that analyzes traffic and other data on mobile websites.

multimedia messaging (MMS). Messages that are sent with audio, video, or graphics included.

multipart MIME format. Email formatting that allows a variety of nontext information to be included in the message. Important to mobile because it helps people receive emails easily on their mobile devices.

off-portal. All mobile web content, applications, and programs that are not specifically offered to cell phone users directly through their cell phone carrier.

on-deck search engines. Search engines provided to cell phone users from their carriers that only display search results that the carrier chooses to show them.

on-portal/on-deck. Content provided by cell phone carriers.

pay-per-call. Advertising model that allows an advertiser to pay for the ad only when a customer calls because of the ad.

pay-per-click. Online advertising model that allows an advertiser to pay for the ad only when a customer clicks on the ad and enters the advertiser's site.

photo-sharing sites. Websites that allow users to upload photos and videos to the Internet so that they can be easily shared with others.

premium SMS. Text messages that are paid for by the consumer, usually a recurring subscription or a pay-to-vote option.

proximity marketing. Marketing that is done specifically to consumers who are in close proximity to the business doing the marketing. Most often associated with Bluetooth marketing.

pull marketing. Marketing that pulls consumers toward the advertiser by attracting them to the content.

push marketing. Marketing that pushes the message at the consumer usually by interrupting the actual content.

revenue-per-customer. Amount of money generated per customer.

search engine optimization (SEO). The act of making your website (desktop or mobile) more visible on search engines to attract more visitors to your site.

send-to-mobile option. A button on a desktop website that when clicked sends content to a mobile phone.

short code. A five- to six-digit code that is used in a text message campaign.

short message service (SMS). Standard text messaging.

split tests. Offering potential customers two or more options and seeing which option achieves better conversion.

text club/subscription. A series of text messages sent out on a regular basis.

text message campaign. Marketing campaign using text messaging as the primary tool.

text message voting. Voting via text message.

text-to-mobile-site link. An embedded link in a text message that when clicked launches the mobile browser and loads the site activated in the link.

text-to-win contest. Contest in which someone wins by texting a particular short code.

tinyurl. A site that takes lengthy URLs (website addresses) and converts them into short URLs that are copied and pasted more easily for consumer use.

transcoding. Process of stripping out all unnecessary graphics and coding from a desktop-built website so that it will be displayed more effectively on a mobile device.

user agent field. A piece of code that is placed in the header of a website and allows the site to "see" how it is being browsed (by full-size computer or mobile device). This lets a site serve the right content based on the device viewing it.

VIP code. A special code that allows users to be placed on a VIP (very important person) list at a venue.

viral marketing. Marketing that is spread naturally from consumers via word of mouth. Often seen in forwarded email.

walled garden. The phrase describing carrier portals that only give certain content to consumers.

WAP push. A phrase that means sending a text-to-mobile link. WAP was once the standard protocol for building mobile sites.

widget. A piece of code on a website that runs a small program on the site. Can be used on mobile devices as well as desktop sites.

About the Author

Kim Dushinski (kimdushinski. com) is the president and founder of Mobile Marketing Profits, a marketing firm that provides mobile marketing education and consulting services to corporations, marketing professionals, and entrepreneurs. As an advocate for smart and effective mobile marketing, she leads workshops and speaks internationally about ways to profit with mobile. She also writes a weekly column at MobileMarketing Watch. com and has been published in publications such as *Search Marketing Standard*.

Kim is a successful entrepreneur with more than 20 years of experience in sales and marketing. She has worked as a marketing director at a travel agency and as a desktop publisher, a business marketing consultant, an Internet marketer, and a partner in a book publicity firm.

Kim lives in Colorado with her husband, Ken, their daughter, Anya, and their dogs.

Index